Dare to Disrupt by Brendan P. Keegan is a transformative and insightful read that delves into the core principles of organizational change. Keegan outlines the eight pillars of transformation in a clear and concise manner, making complex concepts easy to understand through relevant examples and compelling storytelling. As a master at simplifying intricate ideas, Keegan manages to captivate readers of all backgrounds, from new leaders to seasoned executives. His ability to draw from real-world experiences and weave them into the narrative ensures that the book resonates with a wide range of audiences. One of the standouts of *Dare to Disrupt* is its ability to inspire and motivate readers to take ACTION. Keegan's passion for driving transformative change shines through the pages, leaving readers feeling empowered and eager to implement the strategies outlined. Overall, *Dare to Disrupt* is a must-read for anyone who has the passion to fail but the faith to succeed!

BRAD BURGESS
Senior Vice President, Sales & Marketing, Merchants Fleet

A thought-provoking story of how to transform businesses. Will help any business leader think about how they can outperform their market.

JONAH BERGER
Professor, the Wharton School, Penn
Author of *Contagious, Invisible Influence, The Catalyst,* and *Magic Words*

Brendan's exceptional leadership skills and deep industry expertise make him a standout figure in the business world. His ability to navigate complex challenges and identify opportunities for growth is truly remarkable. Through his extensive experience, Brendan has developed a playbook for business success that is both strategic and practical. His insights and methodologies have proven to be highly effective in achieving sustainable growth and long-term success. Whether you're a seasoned entrepreneur or just starting out, Brendan's expertise will undoubtedly help you navigate the ever-changing business landscape and develop a winning strategy. I highly recommend his book as a valuable resource for anyone seeking to achieve extraordinary results in their professional endeavors.

JACK G. FIRRIOLO
Chief Credit & Risk Officer, Merchants Fleet (Retired)

I'm someone who is not naturally comfortable in seeing themselves as a leader, and I worry that I lack that big vision that many leaders have. I love that Brendan writes in such a way that it feels like he's on my level and coaching me to become one of these leaders that he talks of. It's as if he's right by my side believing in me.

EMMA GILMOUR
Business Owner and Professional Racer, McLaren Racing First Female Driver

Keegan's *Dare to Disrupt* is an essential read for anyone serving in a leadership capacity. The clear distinction between evolution growth and transformative growth is eye opening and foundational for those desiring to outperform their industry norms and peers. The examples he provides hit like a ton of bricks and his roadmap for transformative growth is a gift if you have the fortitude and fearlessness to deploy it.

JOHN GERACI
Managing Partner, LGA CPAs and Business Advisors

As an investment banker, a key role we play is telling a company's story. When I met Brendan and saw the impressive transformation that he took Merchants through, the value-creation story had been written, and I knew the story would resonate with investors. *Dare to Disrupt* takes the reader behind the curtain to see just how to lead an industry disruption and business transformation in an easy-to-read playbook—not necessarily easy to execute. I am sending a copy of this book to my CEO clients to support their growth and future.

KRISTOPHER HOPKINS
Managing Director, BMO Capital Markets

Dare to Disrupt outlines the rise and fall of businesses with lessons learned from both. In a fun and engaging format, Keegan intertwines storytelling with sage business advice. This book will leave you feeling inspired to take on your next business adventure, with the toolkit to know how to get started and the skills to level up and disrupt your next venture.

SASHA DIGIULIAN
Professional Climber, Founder & CEO of SEND Bars

A practical guide to business transformation told from the author, Brendan P. Keegan's firsthand experience provides a bird's-eye view of the critical elements to leading a highly successful effort. So many books on this topic focus on the *why*, but this one goes a step further and clearly articulates the *how* in a real-world example. Every transformation is unique but the eight pillars, in some variation, are common tenets to them all. Having lived it, breathed it, and witnessed it personally I can tell you unabashedly, IT WORKS!!!

JERRY PAVELICH
Senior Vice President & Chief Financial Officer, Merchants Fleet (Retired)

Bold and direct, Brendan Keegan makes the complexities of disruptive transformation feel simple and attainable for those who have the fearlessness to tackle it. Whether you're a racer, a budding entrepreneur, or a veteran executive, *Dare to Disrupt: A Playbook for Transformational Business Growth* offers a compelling disruption formula to help drive your vision and fuel your tenacity to defeat the status quo.

JAMES ROE
Race Car Driver and Entrepreneur

Brendan P. Keegan's legacy of business leadership, especially his impressive transformation at Merchants Fleet, informs a range of impactful lessons that he serves up to readers in the form of straightforward and actionable takeaways. Anyone who wants to embrace fearlessness and courage on their personal and professional journey will benefit from *Dare to Disrupt*. Highly recommended for leaders and changemakers aiming to make a significant impact in today's competitive landscape.

TOM POPOMARONIS
Co-Founder & Chief GenAI Officer, Phantom IQ

Brendan Keegan has delivered another thoughtful playbook detailing easy-to-follow steps to achieve transformational business growth. Brendan lays out his eight pillars beginning with Leadership that can help you drive your team or business to year-over-year explosive growth. As then part of his leadership team at Merchants, I saw firsthand how his vision can change your future.

TOM COFFEY
Senior Vice President, Merchants Fleet (Retired)

As one of the investors and bankers behind Brendan and his team at Merchants, I had a front-row seat to see an incredibly impressive and inspirational story of disruption and innovation unfold. *Dare to Disrupt* was a fun and motivating read for me as I had a chance to learn just how the company did it, and the book is written in a way for others to execute their own business transformation. It's a great story, but to see it live and in person was even better! Thank you, Brendan, for sharing the remarkable story in such great detail!

JED HALL
Former Managing Director & Head of New England Region, CIBC Bank USA

As a leader within my firm and an advisor to many entrepreneurs, business owners, and family offices, I found the playbook a digestible approach to creating exponential value in your business. Disruption, transformation, and innovation sound challenging, but in *Dare to Disrupt* Brendan breaks down the eight pillars to disrupt with exceptional clarity. The lessons will be invaluable as I consider the future of my own practice, and I plan to buy a copy for each of my clients.

JAYSON DEANGELIS
Partner & Senior Client Advisor, Ballentine Partners

A great book that serves as a valuable reminder to take a long-range view of your business and a constant review of your competition. Brendan's books always prompt the reader to be on his toes, prepared to adapt, and never fear transformation.

RICHARD DEAN
Chief Executive Officer & Team Principal, United Autosports

DARE TO
DISRUPT

DARE TO DISRUPT

A Playbook for **Transformational Business Growth**

Brendan P. Keegan

Forbes | Books

Published by Forbes Books, Charleston, South Carolina.
An imprint of Advantage Media Group.

Forbes Books is a registered trademark, and the Forbes Books colophon is a trademark of Forbes Media, LLC.

Printed in India by Replika Press Pvt. Ltd.

10 9 8 7 6 5 4 3 2 1

ISBN: 979-8-88750-166-6 (Hardcover)
ISBN: 979-8-88750-167-3 (eBook)

Library of Congress Control Number: 0000000000

Cover and layout design by Matthew Morse.

This custom publication is intended to provide accurate information and the opinions of the author in regard to the subject matter covered. It is sold with the understanding that the publisher, Forbes Books, is not engaged in rendering legal, financial, or professional services of any kind. If legal advice or other expert assistance is required, the reader is advised to seek the services of a competent professional.

Since 1917, Forbes has remained steadfast in its mission to serve as the defining voice of entrepreneurial capitalism. Forbes Books, launched in 2016 through a partnership with Advantage Media, furthers that aim by helping business and thought leaders bring their stories, passion, and knowledge to the forefront in custom books. Opinions expressed by Forbes Books authors are their own. To be considered for publication, please visit **books.Forbes.com**.

MIX
Paper | Supporting responsible forestry
FSC
www.fsc.org FSC™ C016779

To the creators, disruptors, transformers, innovators, and catalysts.

To my wife, Dana, who has served as my spouse, friend, advocate, risk taker, business colleague, teammate, and part-time therapist for over thirty years throughout the many industry disruptions and business transformations, successes and failures, ups and downs. No matter where we were on our journey, she has always provided me with a positive environment to succeed and the commonsense wisdom I often needed to hear.

To my nearly adult children, Kaylie and Patrick, who endured hearing adult conversations early mornings, late nights, weekends, and too often on long drives to lacrosse tournaments and somehow turned those moments into fuel for their own future business endeavors.

CONTENTS

ABOUT THE AUTHOR

Brendan P. Keegan is an award-winning, six-time president and chief executive officer, seventeen-time board director, two-time best-selling author, and the visionary leader behind the bFEARLESS movement. Brendan has raised over $10 billion in capital while leading over 250,000 people and successfully executed six liquidity events.

Today, he serves as co-owner and board member of Andretti Racing, United Autosports, Merchants Fleet, Sky Meadow Country Club, Revolution Armor, ExpressIT Delivery, and Keegan Family Courage & Faith Foundation. His most recent experience was as chairman, CEO, and president of Merchants Fleet where his vision disrupted the industry and transformed the business resulting in 5× top-line growth, 19× bottom-line growth, and 12× enterprise-value growth. As a result, Merchants completed a strategic sale to Bain Capital, Abu Dhabi Investment Authority, and the Leadership Team.

Brendan has authored four books, with his most recent—*Dare to Disrupt: A Playbook for Transformational Business Growth*, published by Forbes Books—coming on the heels of *The FUD Factor: Overcoming Fear, Uncertainty & Doubt to Achieve the Impossible*, which became a *Wall Street Journal* and Amazon bestseller. He hosts the *Fearless Leadership* podcast and is a co-host with Zak Brown, CEO, McLaren Racing, on the *Fast & Fearless* podcast. Brendan's family has a shared mission to give back $10 million to the community through their family foundation to fuel the next generation of leaders.

Brendan received his bachelor's from Rensselaer Polytechnic Institute and his MBA from George Washington University. Brendan is married to his best friend, Dana, and they have raised two fearless kids, Kaylie and Patrick.

ACKNOWLEDGMENTS

I would like to acknowledge the many people who have supported, encouraged, and fueled my fearless leadership journey. A journey that has empowered me to build and lead teams capable of disrupting an industry and transforming businesses beyond my wildest dreams. A journey that has led to the transformational business growth playbook you are now reading.

First, to my parents, who always pushed me to be my best and instilled the confidence in me that my best could be anything I wanted it to be. Their encouragement and belief in me provided me with that initial fuel that set me on this path. Next, special recognition to my wife and best friend, Dana, who has displayed exceptional courage over the last thirty years, twelve moves, and hundreds of ups, downs, twists, and turns. To my kids, Kaylie and Patrick, for reminding me of how the simple things are the simple things. To my career and life mentors Bill Dvoranchik, Val Lyons, John Harris, Gary B. Moore, and Gary Fernandes for believing in me when I struggled to believe in myself.

Next, I want to thank the people who made the disruptions possible. To the Singer family, Gary, Robert, Jeffrey, and Michael, for entrusting me with your life's work and allowing me to bring new ideas to God's country in Hooksett, New Hampshire. To my leadership teams over the past twenty-plus years and specifically to my team at Worldwide TechServices—Steve, Tye, and Mark—and special recognition and thanks to the team at Merchants—Jerry, Jack, Tom, John, Adam, Kristin, Amanda, Diana, Alicia, and Jeanine—for your willingness to push through all the challenges thrown our way from COVID to supply chain and for allowing me to push all of us out of our comfort zones so we could reach new heights together.

To the investors, bankers, and capital market firms who provided over $10 billion to grow, disrupt, and transform (in alpha order): Abu Dubai Investment Authority, Alliance Bernstein, ARES, Bain Capital, Bank of America, Barclays, Bar Harbor, Benchmark Capital, BankUnited, BB&T, BlackRock, BMO, BNP Paribas, BNY Mellon, Broadhaven, Brookline, Canaan Partners, Brown Brothers, Capital One, Centerbridge, Cisco Systems, CIBC, Citigroup, Citizens, Credit Suisse, Deutsche Bank, Doll Capital, Dell Ventures, Eastern, FBR, Fidelity, Fifth Third, Fortress, Goldman Sachs, Houlihan Lokey, InnoCal, Jefferies, JPMorgan Chase, KeyBank, KKR, Kleiner Perkins, Lazard, Legg Mason, M&T, Menlo Ventures, Mizuho, MUFG, Nuveen, Peoples, Piper Jaffrey, PNC, RBC, Regions, Sabre Group, Santander, Silicon Valley Bank, Sprout Group, Sumitomo, St. Paul's, SunTrust, TD Bank, Thomas Weisel, Trinity, Truist, UBS, United, U.S. Bancorp, Webster, Wells Fargo, Welsh Carlson, William Blair, and other capital markets providers that may have mistakenly escaped my memory.

To the authors and professors who have written books and taught programs that sparked ideas and thoughts throughout the transformations I have experienced. Countless times there was a single thought in a book or learning program that came back to me in the middle of a challenge and showed me the way. Here are a few books and learning programs that stand out:

- *Contagious* by Jonah Berger showed me the unique way to make a B2B company infectious.
- *The Tipping Point* by Malcolm Gladwell taught me to incessantly look for the inflection point in new businesses.
- *Crossing the Chasm* by Geoffrey Moore provided the lesson to not give up and to keep pushing for the leap across the chasm.
- *Good to Great* by Jim Collins served as a reminder that endurance matters.
- *Blur* by Bill Kovach reminded me of the role of data and how too much data is simply too much.
- The Innovation by Design executive education program at Columbia University provided the opportunity to learn from professor and consultant Yoni Stern on how to break fixedness.
- The Corporate Sustainability executive education program at Harvard provided guidance on maintaining our focus at Merchants on Doing Well by Doing Good while disrupting an industry.

Thank you to the 250,000 women and men I have had the opportunity to lead into battle in the business world. Thank you for placing your courage and faith in me to be your leader and disruptor. I also want to thank the hundreds of thousands of subscribers to my newsletters and syndicated articles for inspiring me by your viewership, your comments, your likes, and your thumbs-up. A simple comment from someone ten thousand miles away makes me do what I do.

Lastly, I want to thank the team at Forbes, specifically Harper Tucker, for being a beacon of light far beyond the publishing world; Beth Cooper for her edits, research, and ability to help me tell the stories; Nate Best who always provided the right perspective; and Samantha Miller who kept the project rolling and made it possible.

IT'S YOUR TIME TO DISRUPT AND TRANSFORM

When I think of the daunting concept of disrupting an industry or transforming a business, my first thought goes back to my lifelong mantra, *Have the COURAGE to fail and the FAITH to succeed.* To truly disrupt, you must channel your courageous self and instill that same level of courage in others. And to do that, you must have true faith in yourself and your team, and they in turn must have that same faith in you.

My second thought drifts over to FEARLESS leadership, because to channel your courageous self and empower courage in others, you will be called upon to act fearlessly time and time again. Want to start a new business? Engage fearlessness. See the need to shut down an existing business line, division, or service offering? Engage fearlessness. Excited to dabble in a new market and test the waters? Engage fearlessness.

There's no getting around it: fearlessness is required for disruption and transformation. But that doesn't mean it's easy. Too often, we let our own FUD (fear, uncertainty, doubt) get in the way. And no one, not even those considered highly successful, is immune to FUD.

- *We can't do this anymore. We don't know how to grow any differently from our competitors. Should we just sell?* This was the FUD expressed by co-CEOs of a $100 million, family-owned business at a pivotal decision time for their company's future.
- *The team doesn't have the ability to work together to grow the client base to build something great. Maybe we should merge with a stronger firm with aligned leadership.* FUD from a managing partner of a highly successful firm about his own team's ability to transform.
- *Our industry is in decline. Is there even a way to grow the company to re-establish our market value? If there is, I just don't see it.* FUD expressed by a co-managing partner of a blue-chip New York–based private equity firm.
- *How do the Amazons, the Teslas, and the Apples of the world always find ways to stay ahead of their competition and grow faster than the market? They always win. Why can't we?* FUD of a board member of a global, multi-million dollar company.

Experiencing fear, uncertainty, and doubt is unavoidable. It's how you choose to deal with your FUD that significantly impacts the level of fearlessness you are capable of engaging in. And because you can't disrupt and transform without channeling fearlessness—in this book, I will hit on the FUD Factor, but we'll also go far beyond the FUD and dive deep into all aspects of my eight pillars for transformational growth and how you can apply them to your business.

So, what was the real question behind the fears, uncertainties, and doubts of all those high-IQ, highly successful people I quoted before?

How do we transform our business and disrupt what we are doing?

Dare to Disrupt guides you down the path of answering that question for you and your business.

I have spent the last twenty-three years sitting in the corner office as president and CEO of six different companies and have served on nearly twenty boards. The last six of those years I have had the honor and privilege of leading my greatest industry disruption and business transformation at Merchants Fleet. What I have learned through the school of hard-knocks and real-world experience is that everyone wants to build a better company that creates more value for all parties, but not everyone has figured out how to make it happen.

So, as I bring my CEO journey to conclusion to serve more on boards and in an advisory capacity, I have chronicled Merchants' success story in *Dare to Disrupt: A Playbook for Transformational Business Growth* to help others figure out how to make it happen.

Together, we'll go behind the scenes of how Merchants Fleet seized the opportunity to disrupt the fleet industry and set the business on a transformational journey that allowed it to grow from eighth in the industry to fourth in four years with an increase in assets from $500 million to over $2.5 billion and, ultimately, sold for more than 10× its value just a few years earlier.

It was a wild ride. A ride I'm excited to share with you. But first, let's briefly look at what true business transformation is (and isn't). One common misconception is that business transformation is simply increasing an organization's efficiency or implementing new technologies. While these elements can be part of a transformation, true transformation goes much deeper. It involves rethinking every aspect of the business, from leadership and culture to systems and people.

Another misconception is that transformation can be achieved without significant changes to leadership—it can't be done. Why? Because true transformation requires visionary, transformational leadership that is willing to take risks, challenge the status quo, and inspire others to embrace change, and the truth is, if your leadership team currently comprised disruptors and transformers, you wouldn't just be thinking about transforming, you would be doing it.

Additionally, some mistakenly believe that transformation can be achieved quickly or without resistance. The truth is transformation is a complex and often lengthy process that requires patience, perseverance, and a willingness to confront obstacles head-on.

True transformation is the fundamental overhaul of how a business operates, including its strategies, processes, culture, and sometimes even its core offerings. True transformation is about making revolutionary changes that enable a company to outpace its competitors, innovate rapidly, and achieve significant growth.

Transformation is as challenging (and sometimes a bit terrifying) as it is exhilarating, and yes, all businesses, if they are ready, if they have the fortitude to disrupt, if they are fearless in their pursuit, and if the timing is right, can transform. Remember, transformation is not just for the Amazons, Teslas, and Apples!

- *Readiness for Transformation*: Companies must continuously assess their readiness for transformation. This involves evaluating their current capabilities, resources, and the market landscape to determine if they have the necessary foundation for change.
- *Fortitude to Disrupt*: Disruption often requires boldness and courage. Companies must be willing to challenge the status

quo, take calculated risks, and embrace innovation. This mindset can empower them to disrupt industries and create new opportunities.

- *Fearlessness in Pursuit*: Fearlessness doesn't mean recklessness. It's about being daring and resilient in the face of uncertainty and adversity. Companies must have the courage to pursue their vision and adapt to changing circumstances without succumbing to FUD.
- *Timing*: Timing is crucial in transformation and disruption. Companies must be alert for potential opportunities and assess whether the market conditions, technological advancements, and internal capabilities align favorably to act on those opportunities. Acting too early or too late can impact the success of their endeavors.

To make that transformation as painless and as successful as possible, I offer you my eight pillars for transformational growth that I have developed over my twenty-plus years as a transformational leader. In the coming chapters, we'll walk through each pillar in detail and its role in Merchants' transformational journey. Here's a quick glimpse of each of those essential pillars.

- Pillar 1: Leadership. True transformational leadership is essential for driving change. Many companies overlook this, assuming they can transition from a stay-the-course or evolutionary strategy to a transformative one with the same leadership team. I assert that you need to combine three types of leaders in your organization.
- Pillar 2: Culture. The mindset of a stay-the-course or evolutionary strategy differs significantly from that of a transformative one. Shifting from one to the other necessitates a

change in the company's culture. Successfully embedding the innovative and strategic mindset required for transformation takes time—often several years—and instilling the ability to fail is critical and for some, daunting.

- Pillar 3: People. A transformational company requires people with specific skills, experiences, and attributes aligned with its strategic direction and culture. Identifying and addressing skill gaps through assessments, whether through upskilling current employees or recruiting new talent, is crucial for positioning everyone effectively within the organization.

- Pillar 4: Systems. Attempting to introduce disruption and transformation without established systems leads to chaos. Transformation isn't arbitrary; it's based on strategic decisions informed by critical, fact-based information, and built into a repeatable and scalable system.

- Pillar 5: Intelligence (IQ). This pillar involves taking a broad view to identify strengths, weaknesses, and their influences. It's about asking and answering questions to leverage these insights effectively in the transformation journey. It's identifying signals and trends and leveraging your core capabilities to attack them.

- Pillar 6: Emotional Intelligence (EQ). EQ involves understanding underlying values and motives that impact both successes and failures. It also entails self-awareness regarding one's role in the transformation journey and the organization's capacity for change. Without EQ, no transformation is possible.

- Pillar 7: Flexibility. Businesses must remain flexible to adapt to evolving people, environments, motivations, and markets. Transformation requires a blend of forward momentum and adaptability to pivot when necessary.

- Pillar 8: Fearlessness. Transformation requires facing fears, embracing failure, and taking bold actions to disrupt the status quo. It's about confronting the FUD Factor, encouraging a culture where *failure is seen as a learning opportunity, and demonstrating courage to explore.*

You've picked up the book, you've read the introduction. That tells me you must be at least thinking about disrupting and transforming your business. I'm excited for you, and I hope my eight pillars for transformational business growth can help guide you on your transformational journey.

What are we waiting for? Let's get started!

CHAPTER 1

TRANSFORMATION: WHAT IT IS AND WHAT IT ISN'T

Fearless.
Disruption.

Two simple words but core elements to any business transformation and directly correlated to a transformation's long-term success and sustainability.

It was February 2012 when I drove through the early morning snow in Manchester, New Hampshire to have breakfast at a local diner with the chairman of a company I had been a client of for many years. We were both sports enthusiasts and die-hard homers for all the Boston teams, so my expectation was to order a bowl of granola, a glass of chocolate milk, and spend our time serving up everything Patriots, Celtics, Bruins, and Red Sox.

I spotted the chairman in the back corner booth of the bustling diner. As I slid over the aged vinyl covering of the booth's bench, I greeted my old friend with a smile. We caught up on our families' health and activities, and as I moved on to the sports talk, I was politely cut short.

"Brendan, there will be time to talk about the Patriots and Belichick later, this is a business meeting," he stated. I was a bit confused as I was no longer a client or partner and didn't have a current relationship with his company. "We want to recruit you to be our new CEO and transform the company."

I hadn't even ordered my granola and chocolate milk yet and the conversation had already grown intense. I had spent the last twelve-plus years of my career executing corporate turnarounds and business transformations working on behalf of Silicon Valley venture capitalists and New York private equity firms, so I knew what he was asking me to do, and it was right in my wheelhouse—yes, a baseball sports analogy of course.

"Two questions," I replied. "Are you 100 percent prepared to do whatever it takes, even when you have doubts as an owner? And how fast are you looking to grow over the next five years?"

Based on the unscripted and authentic answers to these two questions, I would know if the company and its ownership group had those two words I started with—Fearless and Disruption.

"We are committed to you, and if you can convince us of strategies and approaches that would grow our company above the current market rate of 2 percent and get us into the 5 percent range, we are willing to listen," he said. "We aren't always going to agree, but we are always going to listen and broker a solution."

I had my answer. The company was looking to move on from its historical stay-the-course approach and take an evolutionary approach but clearly not a disruptive one across their industry. The company was looking for incremental growth but not the exponential growth that comes with a business transformation. Incremental growth was a BIG step for the company, and I am sure it was the result of a lengthy and thoughtful decision process among the ownership group and the board of advisors.

However, incremental growth was not the right fit and opportunity for me. How could I tactfully decline this opportunity and leave the relationship intact and unharmed?

"Mr. Chairman," I began, "what a great opportunity for the right person. I can only imagine the many thoughtful hours invested by you and the board to commit to the launching of this new vision and strategic direction for the company, and I am honored you have thought of me as your next Tom Brady to call the plays. However, my background is more suited for transformational growth of 20 to 50 percent with an unwavering commitment to installing a new up-tempo offensive playbook that will disrupt your industry and create tremendous change across your company. All of this requires the staring down of fear, uncertainty, and doubt at every turn. I am good friends with a few incredible field generals who have led similar evolutionary growth companies, and I would be—"

The chairman put his hand up and said, "Let me stop you there Brendan. I thought you were our guy, but that's okay, not everyone is up for the challenge. We all wish you the best of luck." Boom. I had just gotten sacked in the backfield! He shook my hand and off he went.

As I sat in the back corner of that diner, digesting our conversation and sucking down my chocolate milk like a grade schooler, I realized how few people truly understood the differences between stay-the-course, evolve, and transform growth strategies. And, if business owners and leaders don't understand the core pillars required to execute a successful business transformation, they can't grasp the level of fearlessness required to commit to true disruption.

Fear, uncertainty, and doubt are part of all growth strategies, but transformational growth requires leaders to face those fears, uncertainties, and doubts head on. The fear of what success looks like and how that success may render their own skill set less useful, the uncertainty of hiring from outside their industry, and the inevitable doubts that arise when embarking on new strategies and tactics.

It was this very day in 2012, just days after the world-champion New York Giants won the Super Bowl—man was that painful to type—that I decided I would someday write a book about Fearless Disruption and my eight pillars for transformational growth.

And here we are!

What Is Fearless Disruption?

Let's start with disruption in the context of business. Disruption occurs when a company takes a unique or alternative approach to the industry or market segment they are in and significantly outperforms its peer group. Disruptors are all around us.

What made fast food even faster and disrupted the entire model? The drive-through—simple but disruptive, and fast became even faster.

What juggernaut changed the way we rent movies? Online streaming technology. Again, simple but disruptive, and our consumption for renting movies went bonkers.

What revolutionized how we communicate in seconds across the planet? Email. Simple, but completely transformative. And then texting. And then social media. And what's next?

Remember shopping in stores before shopping became available online? By 2027, it's estimated that 23 percent of retail purchases will be made online.[1]

How about printing out AAA TripTiks or MapQuests or pulling into a gas station for directions? Today, we decide which navigation system we want to use be it Waze, Google Maps, or the car's built-in nav system.

Let's even throw out a company that thought of over-pricing (in my opinion) their product but created a cool environment to hang out in that makes you feel special and part of a club. Are you thinking coffee? Me too, but some of you might have been thinking of technology products with unique white cables. Seriously, it's the same damn cable, just white.

In any disruption, there is both simplicity and complexity that drives the change. Let's cover the simplicity first.

These examples are of businesses fundamentally "tweaking" their internal business model with a new, unique, alternative, and/or different approach (e.g., from walking into the restaurant to staying in your car and ordering). It is only after these disruptions occur that they seem like such an obvious next step. Many of these companies continued with their original mode of delivery (e.g., a restaurant with a new drive-through still offered dine-in services).

But why then were they disruptors? To answer that question, we must dive into the complex.

To truly disrupt your market, change your industry, and grow 50 percent faster than your competition, you must transform your

---

1   Kristy Snyder, "35 E-commerce statistics of 2024," Forbes, updated March 28, 2024, https://www.forbes.com/advisor/business/ecommerce-statistics/.

entire business from the inside out. And that, my fellow leaders, is both complex *and* possible. Cue fearlessness.

The single dominating factor of the drive-through, email, online shopping, and navigation systems was the fearlessness with which they executed their vision and implemented these revolutionary changes. I know what you are thinking, some of these weren't revolutionary; they were simple, and you're right. But these simple changes required transformative thinking and an inner fearlessness for the disruptive companies to implement these different approaches. And guess what? For each of these disruptions that we just outlined, there were hundreds that never made it from the conceptual drawing on the whiteboard to implementation, and there were dozens more that were implemented and failed.

I'll take this a step further: the companies that won each of these disruptive wars were by no means the first to think of the ideas. It's not uncommon for one company to have the "transformative idea" but lack the fearlessness to face the doubts coming from inside their own organizations and the uncertainties that couldn't be proven out in a spreadsheet that many of the company leaders were demanding.

Dare to Disrupt is the story of a company I joined six years after my original job offer in a small New Hampshire diner that I turned down in 2012. Yes, I went on to become a board member of that very company and was active in board meetings, throwing out revolutionary ideas and transformative strategies until one day they said, "We are ready, willing, and able" but more on that later.

This playbook, based on my eight pillars for transformational growth, was developed from my own transformational experiences and the transformative powers of companies and leaders I have studied and learned from.

Before we dive into how to apply each pillar to your transformation, let's talk about:

- Why Transform?
- Why Transformations Fail
- The Eight Pillars for Transformational Growth

Why Transform?

Transformation is a fundamental change to what you do, how you do it, and how you go to market. It is revolutionary rather than evolutionary. It is not just growing bigger while doing the same thing or simply diversifying your product or services in line with what you are currently selling. If a restaurant decides to open earlier or stay open later to increase sales, that's a logical, evolutionary step to fill their restaurant more and drive more revenue—it may be a great success, but it's not a transformation of their business. A drive-through that brings in a totally different customer base—now that's transformative.

If your industry is changing, susceptible to change, or a future change is on the horizon and you don't transform, you will not be able to sustain your business. Blockbuster vs. Netflix is a great example.

Blockbuster was at the height of its success in 2004 with nine thousand stores globally and $5.9 billion in revenue. By 2010, they filed for bankruptcy because they stayed the course as they watched their industry be disrupted and transformed around them. While Blockbuster was busy building their brick-and-mortar movie rental empire, Netflix, in 1997, was busy transforming the industry by mailing movies to customers via their subscription service.

Then, in 2007, Netflix transformed how they did business in Canada, converting their subscription service from mailing movies to streaming movies to their customers. In 2010, they opened the service to the U.S., and Reed Hastings, Netflix's then CEO, told his investors, "Three years ago, we were a DVD-by-mail company that offered some streaming. We are now a streaming company which also offers DVD by mail."[2] That's a transformative company who must continue to transform.

If you are an original equipment manufacturer (OEM) of vehicles and you're not investing in electrification, you will be out of business in ten years. GM's leader, Mary Barra recognized the coming fundamental changes to automotive technology and the need to transform GM to meet those changes. In 2018, she shared her vision for zero crashes, zero emissions, and zero congestion. In 2022, Greenpeace East Asia ranked GM number one for its decarbonization efforts.[3] By 2030, LMC Automotive estimates "GM will outshine every other EV manufacturer with 18.3 percent of the market share" because GM has built the infrastructure for true transformation and scalability.[4]

Barra has more than a vision. She has an intentional, strategic plan to make that vision a reality. And there's a third piece of the transformation puzzle we haven't talked about yet: core values. GM's vision and strategic plan align with their core values which include being inclusive, bold, innovative, and doing the right thing, even when it's difficult. Vision, strategic plan, and core values must remain aligned throughout the transformation and beyond (this will be a common refrain throughout the book).

2   Patrick Kariuki, "How and when did Netflix start? A brief history of the company," February 14, 2023 https://www.makeuseof.com/how-when-netflix-start-brief-company-history/.

3   Greenpeace, "Auto environmental guide 2022," https://www.greenpeace.org/static/planet4-eastasia-stateless/2022/09/dd6f236f-auto-environmental-guide-2022.pdf.

4   Q.ai, "GM EV Vs. Tesla: the competition for electric vehicle dominance," September 28, 2022, https://www.forbes.com/sites/qai/2022/09/28/gm-ev-vs-tesla-the-competition-for-electric-vehicle-dominance/?sh=40a9d80c3070.

I bet you thought I was going to highlight Tesla here. Watch out for the juggernaut known as General Motors proving that you can teach an old dog new tricks and turn a battleship like a wakeboard boat!

In today's global and rapidly evolving landscape, companies must always have an eye on the horizon to prepare themselves for the pivots that will be required in the future. Some of those pivots will require a true transformation if they are to stay in the game.

It's important to note that not all companies should or want to transform. In fact, most don't. There are companies who find their course and choose to stick with it for the life of the business. That was certainly true of Merchants Fleet prior to 2018. For fifty-five years, they built a solid business consistently growing at 2–3 percent a year. Most businesses choose, or are better suited for, an evolutionary path. A business that has been steadily growing 5 percent annually for several years may decide they want to increase that growth to 10, 12, maybe 15 percent. They are not looking to make any radical changes. They are looking to improve how they do business and increase their existing market share. Their course of action may be to invest 20 percent more in sales and marketing for a deeper penetration of the market and 10 percent more in product development to create enhancements within their existing offerings, making them more competitive. They have set themselves on an evolutionary trajectory.

In the grouping of companies that want to transform and who think they are ready for and capable of transformation, many often lack the vision, foundation, and fortitude to make it happen. And that brings me to the second part of the transformation equation which you must seek to understand before you embark on disruptive change.

Why Transformations Fail

In his HBR article, "Leading Change: Why Transformation Efforts Fail," John P. Kotter, drawing on his observations of more than one hundred companies over a decade, identifies eight key reasons transformations fail.[5] Before going further, look at the footnote, which is my favorite part of this section. It was written in 1995—why transformations fail is relatively simple and consistent over any time horizon.

- *Not Establishing a Great Enough Sense of Urgency*
  Kotter estimates more than 50 percent of companies fail in phase one of their transformation because they have not created enough of a broad-based sense of urgency, often due to leadership's failure to understand how challenging it is to motivate people to make intentional change and the leader's subsequent lack of commitment in seeing that challenge through.

- *Not Creating a Powerful Enough Guiding Coalition*
  Transformation cannot be accomplished by the CEO or top leader alone. If in phase two, they have not gathered a close coalition of five to fifty people—depending on the size of the company—who have truly bought into the transformation and are committed to its long game, opposition to the transformation—and there will always be opposition—will be difficult to overcome.

- *Lacking a Vision*
  Simply put, "If you can't communicate the vision to someone in five minutes or less and get a reaction that signifies both

---

5   John P. Kotter, "Leading change: why transformation efforts fail," 1995, https://hbr.org/1995/05/leading-change-why-transformation-efforts-fail-2.

understanding and interest, you are not yet done with this phase of the transformation process."

- *Under-Communicating the Vision by a Factor of Ten*
  Telling everyone your vision in a company-wide meeting is not the same as *communicating* your vision. The vison must be embedded in every facet of the company. Top leaders must live the vision and communicate it to everyone in the organization through every available channel on a continual basis. I'd take this a step further and say that in addition to everyone fully understanding the vision, everyone at every level of the company must also be aligned with the strategic direction of that vision.

- *Not Removing Obstacles to the New Vision*
  You can't expect people to follow you if you haven't cleared the obstacles in their path. Obstacles—be they people, processes, or other constraints—must be identified and eliminated. Here again, communication is key—how do you know what your employees see as obstacles if you haven't established an open channel of communication?

- *Not Systematically Planning for and Creating Short-Term Wins*
  If you have communicated your vision well, you have also communicated that the timeline to achieving it is, in most cases, multiple years. Without the intentional creation and implementation of short-term goals that convert to short-term wins, it's impossible to maintain an employee's sense of urgency long-term without seeing progress and benefits along the way.

- *Declaring Victory Too Soon*
  Having a significant win in year one, two, or three of your transformation is great and should be celebrated. But leaders must clearly communicate that this singular win, no matter how amazing, is not the end of the company's transformation journey. Until the vision and transformation are fully embedded in the company's culture—which takes years— declaring victory too early can lead to complacency and a return to the familiar, previous ways of doing business.

- *Not Anchoring Changes in the Corporation's Culture*
  It's critical that leaders make the connections for their employees between the implemented changes and the improved performance. They must see themselves as integral to the vision: "It is who we are and what we do," rather than a temporary, external agent that's creating improvements until the goal is met.

Now, let's move on and talk about the third component you must fundamentally understand: how businesses succeed with the right transformational structure in place. Remember when I said transformations and disruption are both simple and complex? Here comes the complex, so buckle up.

The Eight Pillars of a Successful Transformation

Fortunately, I've had the opportunity to lead the successful transformations of many companies. All of which varied greatly both in terms of size and industries. Through that experience, I have developed a transformational playbook built upon a strategic foundation that supports the eight essential pillars that are required for true transformation. Applying these pillars to your transformation process will remove fear, uncertainty, and doubt by making the complex feel simple. Notice I did not say "become simple." I said "feel simple." Transformation will always be complex. The following eight pillars will help you navigate those complexities.

In the following chapters, we will review each pillar in depth and provide you with a play-by-play of how Merchants Fleet applied these pillars. The intent is to serve as a relevant example for you, the reader, to consider as you begin your transformation journey. We will explore how Merchants went from eighth in the industry to fourth, and from $500 million in assets to over $2.5 billion in under five years. That is truly disruptive and transformative for a company that spent the first fifty-five years going from $0 to $500 million. But trust me, those first fifty-five years were every bit as challenging. Before jumping into each individual chapter, let's look at a high-level overview of the eight pillars of a successful transformation.

Once you have established the company's vision and strategic direction in alignment with your core values (values that must be tested to confirm you are, in fact, honoring them—but more on that later), and everybody, and I do mean everybody, in the company understands it, and you believe you have the fortitude to make the tough decisions, the first question you must ask yourself is, "Do I have the right leadership in place?"

Pillar 1 – Leadership

Transformation cannot happen without true transformational leadership. This is often an oversight and one of the biggest failings of many companies who believe they can move from a stay-the-course or evolve strategy to a transform strategy with the same exact leadership team. It can't be done. If a transformational leadership team was already at the helm, the company wouldn't still be growing 2 or 5 or even 15 percent a year, because true transformational leaders would never be satisfied with that level of growth.

If your leadership has had a stay-the-course mentality for years, all the changes and risk-taking required to transform a company will be not only foreign to them, but it will also make them extremely uncomfortable.

Do you have to change the entire leadership team? No. Based on my experiences, it is best NOT to change the entire leadership team but to instead bring a select few new external leaders into the company, often from more transformative or faster-moving industries. As you bring a few new leaders in and begin the process of transformation, you will see two groups emerge from within your existing leadership team: a group that feels "like the shackles have been taken off" and a group that is extremely uncomfortable and begins to create artificial roadblocks.

Fuel the first group and shine a light on them and work hard to understand the second group. Why are they uncomfortable and/or inexperienced with a transformation? If they are given power, the second group will hesitate and slow you down, and transformation can't exist in that space. While it's true the second group may choose, at some point, to join your transformational journey, and may with coaching, training, and experience be successful, at this juncture, they are better equipped to follow the transformational leaders and fall in line with the transformation process. Remember, fuel the team that wants to be the change.

Transformative leaders are never satisfied with doing well. They are always asking, "How can we do better and how can we grow?" They are the catalysts for change.

While the same eight pillars are applicable to all transformations, they must be adapted to fit the unique attributes of the industry and/or company, and that requires the "right" transformational leader for the circumstance.

Pillar 2 – Culture

The mindset of a stay-the-course or evolutionary business is vastly different from the mindset of a transformative business, and a shift from one to the other requires a shift in the company's culture. For a successful transformation to occur, the innovative and strategic mindset required must be fully embedded in the culture—a process that can take several years. Leadership must have the fortitude to stick with the process and make the tough decisions along the way. To transform, a company must cultivate a culture that attracts and fulfills the individuals who are ready, willing, and able (RWA) to make it happen.

To accomplish this, a transformational leader must:

- UNDERSTAND what the culture is.
- DECIDE what the culture needs to be.
- ASSESS the company's cultural gap between current state vs. future state.
- PLAN actions to accelerate the future state with a focus on:
  - ALIGNMENT: Everyone in the company, from the CEO to the most entry-level team member, must

understand and buy into the strategic direction of the company.

- □ DESIGN: Top leadership must design a process for continuous communication on all levels to assure alignment and a system that supports and incentivizes the growth of every employee.
- □ IMPRINT: Top leadership must live and breathe the transformational culture.

Pillar 3 – People

The strategic direction and culture of a transformational company requires a distinct set of skills, experience, and attributes from its people. Finding, assessing, and developing those people begins with a transformational leader as the head of human resources. One who thinks strategically about how to empower their people, how to level up their people, and how to change their labor force to upskill the skill sets required to transform.

Getting everyone where they need to be, even if that means moving on from the company, must begin with assessments to determine the attributes, skills, and experience required; who has those skills; gaps between current state vs. desired state; and how to fill those gaps by leveling up existing employees and recruiting new talent.

Pillar 4 – Systems

If you attempt to inject a certain level of disruption, transformation, and change into your organization without a system in place, chaos will reign. The transformation process is not random, it's strategically based on critical, fact-based information.

What are the key performance indicators (KPIs)? How will the transformation be sustainable? Are there governance guardrails in place? How will a new product be brought to market? How will success be measured? How will ongoing investment strategies be determined? How will failures be received?

In this transformation playbook, I will outline three critical areas that require a structured system:

1. People Foundation
   - Talent Acquisition and Development
   - Becoming a Talent Magnet
   - High-Performance Culture

2. Growth Engine: Growing Twice as Fast as the Market
   - Brand Equity
   - Sales Strength
   - New Economic Engines

3. Operational Machine
   - People
   - Process
   - Technology
   - Scalability

Pillar 5 – Intelligence (IQ)

This is the process that removes the blinders and takes a wide purview to identify what you're doing well and more importantly, what you're not doing well, and what the influences of those outcomes are. Building a company's intelligence level to read markets, spot trends, identify adjacent markets, and understand core client signals is IQ.

Intelligence quotient is the pillar that asks and answers the questions that enable you to best determine how to leverage those influences to fuel your transformation. A global pandemic is breaking out: what does that mean? Interest rates are increasing: how does that impact your clients and your business internally? Labor shortage is at an all-time high: how do you differentiate your culture to attract new and untapped talent pools? Supply chain shortages are wreaking havoc: how do you source your goods better than your competition?

Without a well-thought-out plan, you risk having those influences slow your transformation, because you can't simply outwork your competitors—that's evolutionary thinking. You must outsmart your competitors, and that begins by fostering and nurturing the overall intelligence level of your organization.

Pillar 6 – Emotional Intelligence (EQ)

EQ is paying attention to what's below the surface to understand people's values and motives that are impacting both your successes and failures. It's also being self-aware of the role you play, the state of the company in your transformation journey, and the capacity and capability your company possesses for change.

Simply put, when asked what my biggest daily decision during a business transformation is, I answer: gas or brake? Transformations demand that you outpace your peer set without leaving your team behind. Some people will be able to keep up, others will find a new gear and learn to keep up, and others won't be able to. In that last instance, you must have the EQ to face the tough decisions and help that person move on from the company. Yes, I did say help, and we will discuss that in the EQ chapter.

You must also know when not to have negative consequences for risk-taking and/or poor performance. It's not black and white. Transformation requires taking risks. If you have established that culture and an employee takes a calculated risk that fails, you must have the EQ to work through that failure while still supporting the culture of risk-taking.

Pillar 7 – Flexibility

When you put together your first transformation plan, it will, at best, be 50 percent accurate. Why? Because you are trying something new, you are changing the game, you are erecting the first drive-through or online store. People, environment, motivations, and markets are continually evolving, and a business must be flexible to meet those changing needs. Transformation requires a continual combination of forward movement and pivots. The previous six pillars all require the flexibility to adjust as needed.

Flexibility requires a mindset that sees challenges as opportunities and is willing to listen, change, and yes, even fail. Perhaps the biggest key to flexibility is continually seeking and encouraging feedback from team members, clients, partners, third parties, and trusted advisors.

Pillar 8 – Fearlessness

The longer you stand at the end of the diving board and *think* about diving in, the harder it's going to be to take the plunge. Transformation is all about:

- Facing the FUD Factor: facing and staring down your fears, uncertainties, and doubts.
- Failing Fast: creating an environment where failure is embraced and encouraged.
- Being Courageous: taking bold actions that create new opportunities and disrupt the norm.

If you create a culture of hesitancy, second-guessing, and fear of failure, you will never gain forward momentum, and without that, there is no transformation.

If you communicate your vision, instill and align core values, articulate and lead the direction of the company, invest in your people, and establish a transformative culture—complete with the systems, IQ, EQ, flexibility, and fearlessness we discussed—you will be following the playbook for a successful market disruption and business transformation. Your team members, partners, and clients will embrace the journey you have invited them to join.

Now, if your vision, values, and direction are not clear, if they are not tangible and understandable, people, even if they want to follow you, will not be able to. How can they if they don't know where you're headed? Set the company vision and then provide your team with a transformation blueprint complete with the eight pillars we outlined, and you will witness one of the greatest achievements of your career. And trust me, it's contagious and addictive.

So, what was the difference between 2012 and 2018 for Merchants and me? Timing. In 2012, the company thought they were ready to transform, but I could see cracks in the alignment: they simply weren't ready, willing, or able to commit to the eight pillars for transformational growth. Then, something changed, and in 2018, I saw an incredible opportunity with the same people to disrupt an entire industry and create a business transformation that led to an extraordinary journey involving more than seven hundred people.

Is your company ready to transform?

Do you have the fortitude to disrupt?

Will you be fearless in your pursuit?

Is the timing right?

CHAPTER 2

GET READY TO TRANSFORM

In early 1999, I moved to Silicon Valley with the dreams of riding the internet bubble. In January 2001, after being on the West Coast for almost two years, I had a front-row seat to the internet bubble bursting. And if you remember those times, it burst hard and fast!

Fortunately, for me, we had just sold the network consulting and internet company that I had moved to Silicon Valley for, and I had accepted my first role as president and CEO of a true tech start-up at an e-commerce and online catalog company. The not-so-fortunate part of the story is that this company was in desperate trouble and only had six months of cash left and a profitable horizon was nowhere in sight. What this company needed was a significant change and not just in revenue and expenses. If the company was going to survive the burst and if I was going to survive my first time as president and CEO, it would need to change its entire business model.

Before I accepted this new and challenging assignment, I must take you behind the scenes of a very special meeting I had with my mentor. We set up an hour-long conference call on an old Star-Trek-looking Polycom phone—there was no Zoom in 2001—and I asked for his honest advice on whether I should take this new job or not. I had sent him one of my typical PowerPoint presentations with all the pros and cons. Within two minutes of listening to me, my mentor cut to the chase and in one single line told me to take the risk and be fearless: "This is the perfect first CEO role. If the company succeeds, you know you've got the ability to run a company. If it does not, then the company reached its natural destination and the company's failure won't ultimately be on your shoulders." Maybe not inspiring words, but true ones.

My first week I had a critical choice to make: which growth strategy was right for my new company? As I discussed in chapter 1, there are only three options for every company: stay the course, evolve, or transform. It didn't take a rocket scientist or a spreadsheet to know that based on the economic times and the company's financial position, my new company's only choice was to disrupt and transform—choosing this strategy is not always so clear, but when you only have six months of cash, sometimes the decision is made for you.

Fast-forward two years and the company was reborn as a business process outsourcing company that had signed more than ten Fortune 500 companies, raised capital in a difficult environment, and had sold to one of its larger competitors. A vastly different business model than the e-commerce tech start-up that existed two years earlier, but our backs had been up against the wall demanding that we take unique and drastic measures or lock the doors forever. Turns out, the FEAR of losing can be turned into a great motivator.

And so began my fearless and disruptive transformational journey.

I spent the next twenty years turning around and transforming five more companies with each one a bit more successful than the previous one. Each experience was an opportunity to hone my skills, learn from my mistakes, learn from other leaders and other successful companies, and further refine my eight-pillars-for-transformational-growth playbook.

Your disruptive transformation must begin with a story, and I encourage you to journal your transformational story as it is unfolding. As you go about transforming your business, you will have many victories, significant losses, risks that played out, and risks that made you question yourself. Always remember to let your vision be your bedrock of strength and the company's core values serve as its cornerstones.

I ended chapter 1 with four questions, and the fact that you are still reading leads me to believe that you answered "yes" or at least "maybe" to some or all of these.

You are ready to transform, you have the fortitude to disrupt, you will be fearless in your pursuit, and the timing is right! Now, let's get you started on your journey by reviewing in greater detail the three growth strategies.

Choosing the Right Growth Strategy

For some businesses, success may mean "if it ain't broke, don't fix it," and they simply want to continue doing what they are doing. I refer to this growth strategy as *stay the course*.

Other organizations desire a little more juice and are willing to inject some change into their organization; perhaps wanting to grow faster, to become more profitable, to expand into a new market. I refer to this growth strategy as *evolve*. This strategy requires a company to evolve as fast or a little faster than their competitors without disrupting how they fundamentally do business.

Some businesses see a great opportunity and truly believe they can put some real distance between them and their competitors if they are willing to change things up. They want to grow twice as fast as their competition, they want to go global, they want to start a new division, and they have an idea of a radical way to serve their clients. Most importantly, they are ready, willing, and able to disrupt and transform how they currently do business. I refer to this growth strategy as *transform*.

Be honest with yourself, pull a few of your colleagues into the conversation, and ask, "What is our growth strategy?"

Let's now define each of these a little more and help you answer, "What's the right growth strategy for my organization?"

Stay the Course

For many companies, stay the course is a highly successful growth strategy. The TJX Companies brand is a great example. You might know TJX as Marshalls and HomeGoods. Their business model of selling surplus, discounted consumer goods from furniture to shampoo for more than forty years has garnered them an expansive and loyal customer base. There's no reason for them to veer off their current course. And honestly, who doesn't love a good shopping experience at HomeGoods, partially because you never know what the selection is going to be? Here's a bit of personal advice for TJX shoppers: if you find that special something and are debating if you should buy one or two more to match—get them all, because it may be the last of its kind to hit a TJX store. I have burned a few Saturdays hopping from one HomeGoods to another across all of New Hampshire and into Massachusetts, to find that one special planter or bed pillow. No doubt many of you have had that same experience.

Choosing to stay the course has worked well for TJX but not so for some other department stores. Bed Bath & Beyond is a primary example who chose to stay the course when the market required them to evolve or transform. There was a time when Bed Bath & Beyond was the best-stocked bed, bath, and kitchen gadget store on the planet. Every college student went to Bed Bath & Beyond to get their dorm supplies—it was a thing—until their "stack it high and let it fly" business model couldn't compete with its competitors who were evolving into online shopping options for their customers with much bigger selections. By the time the pandemic hit, and everyone was shopping online, Bed Bath & Beyond was too far behind to catch up.

At the end of the day, Bed Bath & Beyond did not do enough from a merchandising standpoint and distribution standpoint in e-commerce … They didn't evolve fast enough.

—Bradley Thomas, KeyBanc analyst[6]

So, are you wondering why TJX companies were able to remain successful with their stay-the-course growth strategy while Bed Bath & Beyond was not? Good, you are thinking. Unlike TJX stores, Bed Bath & Beyond did not offer any "unique" products and did not offer them at any "special" price. If you were heading to Bed Bath & Beyond for hotel-brand towels or a KitchenAid mixer, or a Keurig coffee maker, or an L.L.Bean down comforter, you could buy each of

---

6   Khristopher J. Brooks, "3 key mistakes that doomed Bed Bath & Beyond," January 13, 2023, https://www.cbsnews.com/news/bed-bath-beyond-retail-collapse-stores/.

these online, often for a better price, and they were generally guaranteed to have it in stock, and you would receive it in a few days. So, what was the "pull" to drive to Bed Bath & Beyond?

Comfort, wanting to touch and feel the products. But often the downside was Bed Bath & Beyond didn't have the towels in the quantity you wanted, the mixer in the color you wanted, or the down comforter in the right bed size. Now, let's flip to TJX brands; they offer different selections week to week and discounted prices. For many, the experience of discovering a "find" was worth the trip, and that search for treasure—that unique shopping experience—brought their customers back again and again.

Do you see the difference? Are you able to see how product selection, pricing, location, online or in-store, and many other factors come into play when determining the right growth strategy for your business?

There are so many companies, CEOs, leadership teams, boards, products teams, and more who ask themselves what their strategy is and because they lack the true objectivity to be able to honestly answer this question, they say they are evolutionary, because when measured against themselves year after year—they are growing at least 5 percent annually. But in my opinion, the real growth marker is whether you are growing faster than your competitors, because when you are evolving at the same rate or slower than your competitors—the truth is, you are merely staying the course.

Evolve

Let's talk Lego! If you were like me, you had a Lego set when you were a kid and spent hours building, dismantling, and rebuilding things. If you were lucky during the holiday season, you would be gifted additional blocks, so you could build something bigger—and those blocks were virtually indestructible. I remember storing my blue, red, white, and yellow blocks of all different sizes in a big Tupperware box.

In this incarnation of the Lego company, there were only so many Lego sets they could sell to their target audience—young kids—with the build, deconstruct, and rebuild model. As part of their evolutionary path, they made a conscious decision to make three changes: (1) create new ancillary products, (2) target new audiences, and (3) grow the wallet-share of each consumer.

Let's dissect the Lego company's three evolutionary changes.

1. They created new one-time build sets that were very specific. Instead of building a castle from general pieces like I did, today kids and parents build experiences like Hogwarts Castle, Transformers, and The Insect Collection. Lego had successfully created new products using their tried-and-true plastic, snap-together pieces.

2. In my example above, did you notice how I mentioned children and parents were building these more elaborate Lego sets? What I didn't mention was that often there is no child involved at all. In fact, many Lego sets are being bought and built by adults in their twenties, thirties, forties, and beyond who loved Legos as kids and now have the chance to build even cooler things. Lego had successfully targeted new consumers.

3. Core to the Lego company's evolve strategy was to grow their wallet-share of each of their consumers. I can promise you this, my parents bought me two to three generic Lego sets for somewhere in the vicinity of one hundred dollars. But with Lego "experiences," there is less time dismantling and rebuilding with existing Legos and more time buying additional Legos to advance the experience.

I have spent well over $1,000 over the years buying a variety of Lego sets for my son Patrick and daughter Kaylie. The best part of the story? My son and I still buy and build Lego sets annually. Legos moved to an evolutionary growth strategy by packaging their product in new and compelling ways for a broader audience, thus creating much more wallet-share of their consumer base. In fact, we have the daunting McLaren F1 car teed up for our next long weekend—wish us luck!

I am guessing at least a few of you are debating if the Lego company was truly an evolutionary story and not a transformational story. Well, when it comes to their strategy for nearly twenty years, it was evolutionary, but the company did eventually enter a transformation stage, but ONLY after a highly successful evolution. See, the point of this example is to make you think deeply, because often to transform, you must first evolve and learn to change before making the transformational leap. More on this later.

Transform

Walmart was not the first discount retailer, but in 1988, they were the first department store to begin selling groceries, and with that, the first "Supercenter" was born. Walmart transformed how we shop. No more running to one store to buy clothes, another to buy toys, and yet another to buy bananas and bread—heck you can even pick up a couple of trees for your front yard while you're there. Like magic, Walmart made one-stop shopping truly possible. Walmart changed the landscape for discount retailers in a way that benefited consumers. Unfortunately, those benefits came at a cost to specialty retail stores that resided on "Main Street America" and were unable to compete with the giant retailer.

Walmart's disruption of the industry forced their competitors like Target to try and keep up. Something Target eventually did seven years later in 1995 when they opened their first Supercenter with a grocery section.

Walmart made a successful transformation by leveraging their core capabilities, pivoting into new product categories, and dictating the market based on pricing power and consumer belief.

Let's jump into this Walmart transformation more closely and see how they executed this strategy. Walmart:

1. Leveraged two core capabilities: supply chain management, code for buying goods cheaply from their suppliers; and broad distribution network, meaning how many store locations they had and how wide they were dispersed.
2. Pivoted into groceries, landscaping and nursery supplies, and automotive from tires to oil changes and even gas pumps at some locations.

Walmart saw the opportunity to disrupt the industry and transform the brick-and-mortar department store experience. With their size and scale, pricing power, and distribution network, their transformation has been a wild success.

Merchants studied transformational companies and made a decision to disrupt the fleet industry and transform how our clients accessed and utilized fleet services to improve and grow their businesses.

The Start of Merchants' Transformational Journey

In January of 2017, Merchants' board determined that a change was needed—exactly what that change would look like wasn't clear, but by the fall of 2017, Merchants was once again seeking a new CEO.

So, what changed? Why was the timing right now?

Simple answer: age and exit.

The ownership group, a second-generation family represented by four men in their mid-sixties had made the decision that they were not going to pass the company along to the third generation, which led to the realization that they wanted to sell the company in time to enjoy "the fruits of their combined two hundred years of ownership."

The board created a CEO Transition Committee and, as a five-time former president and CEO and a member of Merchants' board of directors, I was asked to join the committee to assist in evaluating candidates and support the development of a transition plan for the new CEO.

Through the process of interviewing eighteen candidates, the family ownership group began to realize that a transformation might be possible. Unbeknownst to me, the four family members had worked with the executive recruiting firm to bring me back as a candidate. It was at this time that I began to consider Merchants as a possibility: this time, they really were ready, willing, and able to transform.

What made the ownership group ready for a transformation *this time*? Same simple answer again: age and exit.

The owners had advanced to an age where they wanted to take one last "shot" at fueling their fifty-five-year-old company to new heights. And exit, they had recognized that if this fuel was possible, they would be rewarded with a greater valuation at exit.

On January 1, 2018, I became the transformational CEO they were looking for, and Merchants set out on a path to disrupt the fleet industry and build a single fleet management company that hadn't been built before.

Disruption Formula: Opportunity, Vision, Transformation

Every disruption formula includes opportunity, vision, and transformation. In some cases, it is the opportunity that presents itself first, and in others, a vision forms and then you begin to look for opportunities to achieve that vision. Whichever comes first, they must both exist before transformation can take place. It's important to note that there are industries in which opportunities to disrupt may not exist in that moment—if Netflix's vision for directly sending movies to your TV had been conceived before the technology for streaming was available, the opportunity would not have been present for them to act on that vision—and if that is the case with your business, it's best to recognize it early and focus on developing your evolutionary growth strategy until the right transformative opportunity arises.

Once you've identified the opportunity to achieve your vision, it's time to start the engine and develop your transformation roadmap. For Merchants, disrupting the fleet industry began with a vision followed by opportunity, and very quickly, they were intertwined and became one.

When I took over the helm as CEO, Merchants comprised seven different companies, each with a different name, a different team, and in most cases, in a different building across or down the street or even across the country. There was no physical, technological, or logistical centralization. It was a siloed system with no intentional crossover between them. I had been a client for many years before I was a board member, but it wasn't until I joined the board that I became aware of all their other services. When I asked how come as a client, I didn't know about the other services, the response was, "You weren't a client of that division."

"Is it the client's job to understand your company's organizational chart and to figure out if the company offers other services they may want to use?" I asked. That mindset and organizational structure had enabled successful stay-the-course growth over the past fifty-five years, but it would not allow for scalable and sustainable growth moving forward. So, from day one, my vision was to build the "confederation" of Merchants companies into one single centralized company that would offer all clients all services. I am confident there are a few of you reading this and identifying this highly relatable and prevalent practice of different sub-brands or silos within your own company.

What was the opportunity for Merchants? There were eight national long-term leasing companies and another ten short-term leasing and rental companies, but there was not a single company that offered rentals, short-term leasing, and long-term leasing. All the veterans within the industry cited many reasons why this was true: "they are different business models," "you need different systems," and "they are operated differently." The next statement was the most challenging for me, "They are different mindsets for leaders to manage."

The opportunity was to build the first and only fleet management company that offered rentals, short-term leases, and long-term leases to all their clients nationwide. If you are from outside the fleet industry, you may be thinking the same thing that I was thinking during my first year at the company as CEO—this doesn't seem crazy or wild; it seems logical, and you would be 100 percent right. But remember the drive-through example from chapter 1? It seems logical, but for the fast-food industry at that time, it was quite radical.

Next up was creating a simple vision that team members, clients, and prospects could understand and that demonstrated our uniqueness. As a fleet management company, we supported our clients moving "things" using cars, vans, and trucks, and our clients spanned over twenty different industries from universities and pre-schools moving people, to courier and logistics companies moving goods, to dental companies providing services. We wanted our vision to represent our new approach of offering rentals and leases of any type, and so, our vision was born:

ENABLE THE MOVEMENT OF PEOPLE, GOODS, AND SERVICES FREELY

ENABLE represented how Merchants did not move anything, but we supported our clients' ability to do so.

MOVEMENT represented the vehicle "moving," but we did not want to limit ourselves to saying vehicle in case we wanted to enable more types of transportation in the future.

PEOPLE, GOODS, & SERVICES represented that we were industry agnostic, meaning we were not tied to any specific industry, and we could enable any industry.

FREELY was our magic word. It represented any rental or lease of any term; you could rent or lease from us freely, on your terms.

Our competitors could look at the first eight words and say, "We do the same thing," but no one in our industry had figured out the ninth word, *freely*. That opportunity and vision led Merchants on a wild transformation over the next four years.

Merchants' go-to-market strategy was a combination of the Lego company by creating new product offerings that were adjacent to existing capabilities and Walmart by disrupting the long-term fleet leasing market by being the only company that could also do rentals and short-term leases. Walmart had truly made one-stop shopping possible. So, think of the new Merchants, or as we called it internally, Merchants 2.0, as a great big Walmart Supercenter.

The third part of the disruption formula—Transformation—will be discussed in detail over the next eight chapters as we delve into the eight pillars for transformational growth. But to give you the advance headline, the opportunity that we uncovered, the vision that we created, and the transformation we executed allowed us to grow from eighth in the industry to fourth in four years with our assets growing from $500 million to over $2.5 billion.

What was the strategy and the strategic direction behind this exponential growth? Simple: FUEL!

FUEL: Fuel, Unique, Electric, Leader

We dubbed our Strategic Direction with the acronym *F.U.E.L.4*:

F	**Fastest**-growing fleet company in North America
U	**Unique** business model with differentiated value to our clients
E	**Electric** vehicle evangelist with progressive ESG approach
L	**Leadership** positioned to fuel a $2.5 billion company
4	**4th** in the industry

If you are thinking about developing a transformational journey for your company or are in the midst of your journey, please take note of two important things in this chapter.

1. Merchants' vision was nine words and very simple to remember and even easier to understand.
2. Merchants' strategic direction was represented by a single word that was relevant to the fleet industry.

Making something complex is easy; making something simple is difficult. Making Merchants' vision simple and its strategic direction even simpler was challenging work, but the benefits were tremendous because every team member would come to understand the journey we were on together. The simplicity also made Merchants a magnet for new talent.

Simple for Clients and Prospects to Understand

Clients like simple. They like to know who you are, what you do, and what makes you different or better. For Merchants, this really hit on the "U" in our strategy: Unique. Our business model was unique by offering both rentals and short-term leases similar to Budget, Enterprise, Hertz, Ryder, and Penske and long-term leases similar to Element, Wheels, ARI, and Donlen, a division of Hertz. When a client did business with Budget, Hertz, Enterprise, Ryder, or Penske, they could only do rentals and short-term leases. And when a client did business with Element, Wheels, ARI, or Donlen, they could only do a long-term lease. But almost every client had a need to do both.

Merchants became the only company in North America that offered both rentals and short-term leases along with long-term leases. And you, just like many of our prospects, are wondering, "why didn't everyone offer both?" Because doing both is very complex.

Let's dissect Hertz and Donlen along with Enterprise. As you probably know, Hertz offers rentals to both consumer and commercial clients. What you might not know is they owned a long-term leasing company by the name of Donlen. Much like Merchants prior to our transformation, they ran these two companies separately with different names, sales teams, organizations, and services. Even though they were owned by the same company, they presented themselves to clients as two separate companies to do business with. Sound familiar? This is how Merchants was for over fifty-five years. Now, let's turn to Enterprise who also had Enterprise Rentals that many of you are familiar with and owns Enterprise Fleet, which you may not have heard of. In this case, they used the same name, but they were separate companies with separate sales teams, organizations, fleets, and their clients were unable to work with them seamlessly for their entire fleet. Again, much like Merchants' pre-transformation. So, why couldn't they take the same approach as Merchants? Two missing elements: fearless leadership and a disruptive mindset.

Complex and Challenging for Team Members to Execute

Looking back on Merchants' disruption formula, the vision was to enable movement *freely*, and the strategic direction was to have a **U**nique business model which was the launching pad to the transformation.

So, freely and unique were two critical cornerstones of Merchants' transformation, and these two cornerstones allowed the company to become the **F**astest-growing fleet company in North America. Are you starting to see how all of these are tied together? Let me make one more connection for you. In 2021, three years after Merchants' new vision was launched, one more word was added: *responsibly*. Well technically, two words: *and responsibly*.

Enable the movement of people, goods, and services freely *and responsibly*

Responsibly was added to the vision to increase the Electrification and ESG portion of Merchants' strategic direction. Merchants lived in an industry that was not fast to market or fast to change, and we wanted to continue to demonstrate to our clients that we were a progressive-thinking and forward-looking company.

Lastly, as Merchants doubled from $500 million to $1 billion and then again to $2 billion in under four years, the last part of our strategic direction, Leadership, became vital. Merchants' fastest growth, unique business model, and progressive electrification and ESG thinking were making us leaders within our industry, but more importantly, Merchants was developing the leadership ranks within the company to properly govern and manage the vision, strategy, and growth.

Putting all these pieces together is the complex part. While Merchants was able to truly build something that did not yet exist, it also stretched our team and our internal capabilities. As we begin to delve into the eight pillars for transformational growth, I encourage you to take specific note of Pillars 1, 2, and 3: Leadership, People, and Culture. If you are ever going to do something amazing in any company, I firmly believe you must build the leadership foundation first, invest in your people, and create a strong culture.

Values-Driven Transformational Leadership

Assessing and investing in the capabilities of your leaders to fully engage in the transformation is essential and it all starts with values. Your executive leadership team must not only be aligned on the vision and the strategic direction, but they must be in lockstep with the company's values. Nothing will slow a company down more than a leadership team that does not lead from the same core values. And nothing will accelerate your growth and transformation faster than when your team is fully aligned with the company's core values.

When a transformation kicks off, you can't predict who is and isn't going to make it, who is going to excel and who is going to struggle, who is going to be a raving fan, and who will need to be transitioned out. There may be a person you don't think will be able to make the shift, because they have worked in the "stay-the-course" leadership mindset for their entire thirty-year career. Or you may bring in a superstar from another company who you are convinced is going to hit it out of the park with their progressive thinking. In my case, both predictions had opposite outcomes: one of Merchants' thirty-year veterans had been waiting for this opportunity to prosper and was the one to hit it out of the park, while one of the new superstars I brought on board never quite fit the culture and therefore couldn't get the job done, and we had to move on from each other.

The people process takes time and effort. At the end of the first week, first month, maybe even the first quarter, you still won't know everyone who is going to commit to the journey long term, but you keep investing and assessing. You keep working the bell curve.

The Bell Curve

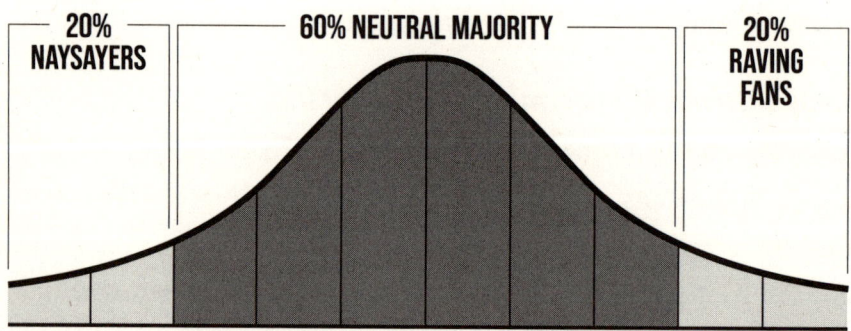

Right out of the gate, 20 percent of the people jump on board and become raving fans and 20 percent of the people are "I'm not doing that," or "That's not possible." The remaining 60 percent are uncertain and are the core group you need to invest in. They need more clarity on the destination or more information on how they will get there or how they will benefit. It will take time and effort to get them to decide. You must stick with it, because if the company is truly going to disrupt and transform, you can't do it as a CEO. You can't do it as a leadership team. You can only succeed if every person in the company is on board.

To that end, you must let every single person, as an individual, decide to jump in or jump out. You want people to join the transformation journey because they want to, not because they feel they must. It's important that they believe in the journey and can visualize their role and reward in it.

To this point, I have had you ask yourself if you are ready, willing, and able to transform, have the fortitude to disrupt, and the courage to be fearless in your pursuit. I have outlined the Disruption Formula: opportunity, vision, and transformation. Now, let's jump into how erecting each of the eight pillars will lead to your company's successful transformation. And it all begins with establishing a foundation of Transformational Leadership.

CHAPTER 3

PILLAR 1: LEADERSHIP

"How come you haven't done anything about our technology leader? He just doesn't get our vision and have the commitment we need." That's what a twenty-something individual contributor in my first transformation company asked me. The week before when the younger individual asked if we could meet, I thought he was seeking my advice on how he could advance in the company. Boy, was I wrong!

The leader in question was in our technology department and was leading the change to a new enterprise architecture for the backbone product that drove our company. "What are you thinking? Why are you so convinced they don't get our vision? Questioning their commitment is a real statement," I replied.

"They just don't get it," he said, "and they have no real intention to make the transition to being a cutting-edge technology-enabled company. They are taking a much more conservative approach, using old technologies, and they are not willing to take a risk on any new technologies."

Turns out, this young team member was right. This leader wasn't simply playing it safe; they weren't getting our vision of being a technology leader, and they simply weren't going to. A tough lesson for me at the time: one that cost our company four to six months of progress and millions of dollars in application development. I learned a lot of leadership lessons that day, including the importance of 360-degree communication, the lack of which, in this instance, kept me from seeing the issue in the first place. But equally essential was learning the importance of assessing just how ready, willing, and able the members of any leadership team are and then making the tough decisions.

When I was able to sit back and review what had happened, I realized I hadn't had an honest conversation early on about what was required and whether this individual's skills, experience, and attributes matched up. He had been the leader of that area for many years, but that didn't mean he was the right one to carry us forward through the transformation. I totally underestimated the attributes' component. This person was not willing to make a mistake, take a risk, or try something new.

Building the Right Leadership Team

If you are transitioning from a stay-the-course or an evolve strategy to a transform strategy, you must be willing to recognize that your existing team likely isn't going to be the EXACT team that gets you through that transformation. You will need other voices from within the organization, voices from outside the organization but within the industry, and voices from outside of the industry. Please notice I did NOT say start over with a new leadership team. This is a mistake many people make, and far too often, new CEOs think that bringing in all external voices—oftentimes voices they have worked with before—is the best option. I am an ardent believer in keeping as MUCH of the existing leadership team as possible, promoting from within, recruiting top talent from your industry, and bringing in true outsiders from other industries. But notice the progression: existing team, within the company, within the industry, and then outside the industry.

Fast-forward to September 2022. I was the keynote speaker to five-hundred-plus clients, bankers, investors, and partners at Merchants' annual fleet summit. When I was planning this keynote, my marketing team came to me and said people were asking if I would be willing to talk about the company's transformation, as we had just been sold a month earlier. Those requests determined what my topic would be for the fleet summit: The Eight Pillars of Business Transformation. I introduced the pillars and really emphasized Pillar 1, "Building a successful business transformation begins with transformative leadership." I put up a slide of my leadership team and began to explain how the team came together.

- Four members of our leadership team had been with the company between seventeen and thirty-three years—they had institutional knowledge.
- Three members of our leadership team had been recruited before I arrived and came from our competitors. They came from outside the company, but inside the industry, and they brought best practices from within the fleet industry and new ways of operating.
- Three members of our leadership team were recruited after I joined the company, and each came from outside the fleet industry and brought their own unique perspectives to the table from leading technology and consulting firms.

So, why does this mix matter? Well, when we started to problem solve together, the homegrown Merchants leaders would say, "Hey, here's how we've done it." The new leaders from within the industry would say, "Here's how the best companies in this industry do it." And the newest leaders from outside the industry would ask, "Why do we do it that way?" or even "Why do we do that at all?" They may have come from a tech industry, a financial services industry, or a consulting company and had solved the same problems with a different approach, and it is that spirit of collaboration and open sharing of ideas, perspective, and experience that helped fuel Merchants' ability to innovate, disrupt, and transform.

Now, I also want to tell you a little more about this leadership team that I shared with the audience that day. The leadership team had ten people and only three were new. I was one of the three new, and I brought two other new leaders to the company. The other seven were already with the company. Now, we did move people around, promoted from within, and recognized that a few existing team members were not going to make it. I also recognized that we had a real diversity issue. All the leaders before I joined were males. By the end of my first year, we had a team of ten and five were females which fueled a whole new recruiting strategy.

"If you can't commit," I told my fleet summit audience, "to true transformational leadership, your transformation will fail."

As soon as I finished my keynote address, one of our top clients from a Fortune 100 company approached and asked if they could get a copy of my presentation. He explained that his company was in the middle of a transformation and based on my playbook and how I looked at transformation, he now felt that they were positioned to fail, and he wanted to meet with his executive team to reassess.

I let him know that there were multiple ways to build the right transformative leadership team and the breakdown I presented is what worked for Merchants.

"Yes, but your comment about how challenging it is to expect that a leadership team made up of only people who have grown up in the company and share one mindset can suddenly change and transform to a different mindset really hit me," he said. "It's so clear to me now that we need to bring in some people from different industries who can help solve problems in new ways."

Transformational Leadership Defined

I define leadership as the willingness to accept responsibility to organize a group of people to achieve a common goal.

Let's break down the key components of that definition:

- *Willingness* is having or showing the ability and desire to respond without being forced to and without delay.
- *Accept* is having a favorable opinion or to take something upon yourself.
- *Responsibility* is having to do something because of a prior agreement and being worthy of another's trust or confidence to get it done.
- *Organize* is putting things, tasks, or people into a particular arrangement.
- *Group* is usually a small number of people or things considered as a unit.
- *People* are folks, a society, community, masses, populace, family, or the public.
- *Achieve* is to obtain a goal through effort, to carry through to completion.

- *Common* is belonging or relating to the whole. It is also something that is done by a group of people.
- *Goal* is something one hopes or intends to accomplish.

My definition of transformational leadership has one exception. The goal must be extraordinary.

The willingness to accept responsibility to organize a group of people to achieve an extraordinary goal.

Ordinary is evolution. Extraordinary is transformational, and that requires people who are willing to give that extra, to reach higher, to be *willing* to elevate themselves and those around them. They must also be *ready* and *able* to achieve the extraordinary goal. This is where skills, experience, and attributes come into play. Some people may not be ready because they lack the experience and/or skills, and some of those people will be able to gain the experience and develop the skills necessary to get them ready and able. Others may never be able to acquire the skills needed—they will never be able to achieve the extraordinary goal no matter how much experience or training they receive.

There will be team members who have the necessary skills and experience but don't possess the attributes of a transformational leader. Here are four key attributes that I look for in my leaders:

- Intellectual curiosity
- Open-mindedness
- Collaboration
- Trust

Intellectual curiosity is the desire to learn about the world around you, to ask "why" and "how" with purpose. Research indicates a connection between curious behaviors and adaptive behaviors. Those with a curious personality exhibit a higher tendency toward positivity, playfulness, unconventional thinking, and a tolerance of anxiety and uncertainty:[7] critical traits for a leader to practice and to encourage in those they lead.

To have intellectual curiosity is to practice *open-mindedness*, because to have intellectual curiosity is to be open to new ideas, challenge existing ones, and listen to the thoughts and ideas of others. Leaders who encourage intellectual curiosity by asking how and why and listening to the hows and whys of others with an open mind and without judgment, empower their team to *collaborate* freely and build *trust*—trust that they will be listened to with respect and without judgment, trust in their team members to get the job done, and trust from their team members that they will also get the job done.

Establishing the Leadership Foundation

I began building the foundation of what would become Merchants' senior leadership team from day one in January of 2018. It wasn't until December that same year that I was confident that our senior leadership team was established. Building a solid leadership team does not happen overnight. It requires time, thought, and intention. It requires a change-management approach that allows time to assess each leader's skills, experience, and attributes, how well they adapt to change, and how well they collaborate as a group. It's important to allow each

---

7   Todd B. Kashdan, Ryne A. Sherman, Jessica Yarbro, and David C. Funder, "How are Curious People Viewed and How Do they Behave in Social Situations? From the Perspectives of Self, Friends, Parents, and Unacquainted Observers," *Journal of Personality 81, no. 2 (2013): 142–154,* https://www.ncbi.nlm.nih.gov/pmc/articles/PMC3430822/.

leader a chance to make it through the transformation. It can be tempting to make assumptions about who will and won't make it, but I strongly recommend that you don't act on those assumptions. As I shared in chapter 2, those assumptions about who will be a superstar and who won't be able to jump on the transformation train can be dead wrong. Be patient. Trust me, I am not a patient person, but when it comes to transformational leadership, patience is required.

Throughout 2018, we began talking about the company differently, we rebranded the company, and we built our transformational leadership team. Over the course of that process, we had three senior leaders who didn't make the transition. One had the skills and experience but lacked the right attributes; they were unwilling to listen to and acknowledge the ideas others brought to the table. We had another leader who was a strong leader and was willing to change, but we just couldn't make their skills and experience match what we needed in a transformational people leader. We were able to promote another leader from within the HR team who had the skills, experience, and attributes to see that function from a transformational perspective. And we had a third person who just didn't fundamentally believe in our transformation. It wasn't that they couldn't develop the attributes. It wasn't that they didn't have the skills or the experience. They just weren't buying into the vision. It takes a strong person to be able to say that to you, and I'm glad they did. It allowed me to have that conversation about the right fit and help that person move along in their journey.

At its foundation, every member of your leadership team must fundamentally believe in the vision and believe they can accomplish what they have never accomplished before. They must have the courage to fail and the faith to succeed. (You will see this a few more times, I promise.)

Now, as all these changes were coalescing, what wasn't changing much that year was our profit and loss (P&L) statement. There was no transformational revenue growth in the first year, because for explosive growth to happen, you must first lay the foundation. That foundation begins with the right leaders. If you don't have a team that's willing to listen, change, and think in new ways, no matter how great that 30 percent growth idea is, it will never be executed. Do not tell your board, investors, and partners that your transformation will garner 30 percent growth in year one. It's not going to happen. Be patient. Trust me, I know how hard it is for leaders who are driven to disrupt and transform to have patience with the process—but I know from experience that patience is essential for scalable and sustainable growth. Are you noticing this patience theme? Remember, it is year one. This changes in later years but is critical at the start.

Now, once the right foundation is laid, magic will happen, and it will happen quickly, because engaging in a disruptive and transformative process will open your mind to opportunities and possibilities everywhere—that doesn't mean that they are all ones you should pursue, but it creates an undeniable synergy that moves you forward in new and unexpected ways.

In 2018, we had been offering short-term rentals for summer camps for several years, so we asked, "Why aren't we doing short-term rentals in last mile e-commerce?" (Last mile in e-commerce is the movement of goods from a transportation hub to the final delivery destination—generally a home or office.) Last mile is a much bigger market for short-term rentals than summer camps. The leader in charge of that, who had been there for thirty years leading the stay-the-course strategy, could have easily said, "Nah, I don't believe in last mile. I don't think that's a good market." But because we had built the transformational foundation and mindset, because he knew it was okay to try things even if that meant failure, he instead said, "Wow! Why haven't we gotten into the market before? Let's do it."

We entered the last mile e-commerce market in Q4 of 2018 with 289 cargo vans on the road. We went from our existing 1,500 short-term rental vehicles (non-e-commerce markets) to 1,789 vehicles in three months. That was a quick win for Merchants, and we were high-fiving each other like we had just invented sliced bread. That type of success breeds the "how can we do more of that" thought process. In 2019, we did 3,000; in 2020, we did 5,000; in 2021, we did 10,000; and now five years later, we have nearly 15,000 cargo vans and trucks on the road serving the last mile market. What if at the outset of our last mile program, the thirty-year veteran had been an obstacle and said "no" to the last mile market? What if he did not have the attributes necessary for change? What if he was too set in his ways and had said, "This isn't how we do things at Merchants"? I gave a snapshot of this quick win and five-year roadmap so you can truly understand the importance of leadership buying in. It really does all begin with Pillar 1. If Mary Barra, who had been with GM her entire career, had embraced a fixed mindset and refused to make transformational changes at GM—would the giant automotive company have been able to survive? I'm betting they wouldn't.

How we entered the last mile e-commerce market and how quickly we grew in that space was a direct result of having the right leadership foundation and mindset in place. When we constructed our strategy of collapsing seven businesses into one, senior leadership became a much more collaborative team. So, when we launched last mile, it wasn't one person in one business unit doing it by themselves. The enterprise involved a truly collaborative and innovative approach. We had a head of marketing who was building marketing plans. We had our head of recruitment search for people with the right skill sets and experience. We had our head of technology developing our technological capacity to enable that new service offering. We had our head of operations assess how to adapt the registration and maintenance of our vehicles accordingly and re-engineer our customer call center for our last mile clients.

The pursuit of a business transformation is very much a team sport. Every member of the team must be behind it. That doesn't mean people don't question it during the decision-making process, but once the decision has been made, you must move on all fronts. Now, three or six months down the road, you may determine that it wasn't a good decision and pull out—but when you're in it, everyone must be all in.

Your senior leadership team is responsible for developing the organization's leadership. They must communicate what the vision is and how it will be successfully achieved from their vice presidents to directors, managers, and every employee. It really does require all the front-line managers to be on board, because they are the daily communicators with your individual team members. If you have a manager not on board, you will have a team of individuals not on board.

Last mile e-commerce was new for everyone, and it was hard and was a bit chaotic as we worked out the people, systems, and processes to make it happen. If we hadn't had that manager three or four levels down who believed in the vision and embraced the positive mindset of "Hey, just get them on the road, and we'll figure it out later," they would have created roadblocks, and we may have only put 89 vehicles on the road in Q4 instead of 289, and five years later, have 1,000 and not 15,000 trucks on the road—a monumental difference.

Once the vision was understood at all levels of the company, and we had a growing number of people who were ready, willing, and able, we began to fill the gaps and build upon our leadership foundation. The quick wins we experienced accelerated the transformation process.

What's something "new" you can do, something that creates momentum, something tangible that people can get behind?

With the transformative leadership foundation in place, we began to lean into leading, managing, and coaching up and down the organization to fuel Merchants' growth across all aspects of the business.

Lead-Manage-Coach Model

When I made the decision to be the transformational leader for Merchants, I committed to creating a leadership academy for directors and managers that focused on how to lead, manage, and coach their teams. I also committed myself to being the academy's leadership trainer. Was committing my time as CEO to four hours of leading a training session every month the best use of my time? Some may argue it wasn't, but I would do it again given the chance. I had such clarity of vision for the leaders of our company that even though I am not a trainer by nature, that vision coupled with my transformational experience made me the right leadership trainer in that moment.

My role in the leadership academy provided me with the opportunity during the very early and critical stages of Merchants' transformation to interact closely with every leader across the company, from finance, sales, operations, human resources, technology, and more. It allowed me to inject a leadership model of "lead-manage-coach" across the company at hyper-speed. For me, those opportunities were some of my biggest wins. I remained the leadership trainer through 2020. I was able to step back in 2021, because virtually every leader in the company was living and breathing the lead-manage-coach model every day.

There were many times in the hours before a leadership academy session when I would be asking myself, "Should I really be doing this?" I can honestly say that at the conclusion of every single session, my answer was "Absolutely," because in every session, there was some magic that happened, some dots that got connected, or a leader that was neutral on our vision who converted to being a fan. I also had a few people after sessions determine that they were no longer a fit for the company, and that was just as beneficial.

Throughout this chapter, I have talked extensively about what it means to lead. Now, I want to talk about what it means to manage and coach.

Manage

While leading is all about setting the vision and the path to achieve it, managing is the process of planning and organizing the resources and activities to effectively and efficiently achieve the goals that lead to the vision. At the forefront of that process is identifying the key performance indicators (KPIs) that will inform when your strategy has taken root to when your goal has been successfully achieved and every point in between. The data gathered from a company's KPIs provide quantifiable measurements that are used to gauge a company's strategic, financial, and operational performance.

As data based on KPIs are gathered, a performance dashboard provides a visual status of an organization's KPIs from a company-wide view all the way down through departmental, process, and individual view. The dashboard allows every employee to see how their tasks and activities help to realize the goals of an organization.

One of our initial KPIs was how many cargo vans we put on the road. A few weeks/months into entering this new market, we added two new KPIs: how many cargo vans we took off the road and how long each vehicle was leased and on the road. When the data indicated that we had moved from 0 to 289 units on the road in three months, we determined it was time to invest more resources into the last mile program. That insight was garnered from a lagging indicator—what had already happened.

- *Lagging indicators* reflect what has already happened this week, month, quarter, or year. Think about a few practical examples like your revenue for last year, your attrition rate of your employees, the number of wins and losses of your favorite sports teams. Most organizations spend a high percentage of their time reviewing lagging indicators and that is normal. Look at most of the reports you receive, the dashboards you have at your company (if you are lucky), or the trackers you have on your spreadsheet. Lagging indicators are what you see in your rearview mirror. They are reactive measurements.

- *Leading indicators*, on the other hand, are what you see through your windshield. By seeing what's happening in real time, leading indicators help predict what you *will see* in the rearview mirror next month, quarter, and year. Let's think about some practical leading indicators. How many prospects visited your website, how many résumés were received for an open position, how many clients signed up for a new service or product you offered? All of these are leading indicators or what most likely will happen in the future.

Take a look at the following comparison of leading and lagging indicators.

LAGGING INDICATORS ARE...

- used to measure goal accomplishment and historical performance
- easy to measure
- hard to influence
- 80 percent of measurements and management reports
- **Examples:**
  - Total Return Merchandise Authorizations (RMAs)/Lates
  - Revenue
  - Customer Service Events

LEADING INDICATORS ARE...

- used to predict goal achievement
- more difficult to measure
- easier to influence
- less than 20 percent of management reports
- **Examples:**
  - Number of sales touches
  - Average handling time
  - First contact resolution

What happens when too much time is spent on lagging KPIs and not enough time on leading ones? Let's look at customer service calls as a leading indicator. If you're receiving five calls per client per month asking for assistance with a product issue, you're probably wondering if you have a winning product. But if you couple that with a lagging indicator of high client satisfaction with the product, something's not adding up. This is the point where too often leaders see the revenue decline or the high service call rate and start solving for the wrong problem before exploring what is really going on.

Instead of jumping in with a solution, take the time to understand the inter-play between the indicators. In this instance, why were there so many issue calls for a product that so many clients liked? It may be that the product is as great as reflected in your customer satisfaction surveys, but the company's product training for new clients and new users is inadequate. If you don't address the issue with your new clients and users, your client satisfaction will decrease in the future, which will negatively impact future sales and revenue.

Let's look at how Merchants leveraged its leading customer service indicators just as the last mile program was ramping up. The number of cargo van drivers inquiring about things like where to go for an oil change and my favorite, "Where's the key?" was too high. These leading customer service indicators suggested that we needed to do a better job connecting our customers with our Merchants Fleet app, because not only was having to call in frustrating for our customers, answering every one of these calls was more expensive than providing the drivers the resources to solve the problem themselves. With the information from that leading indicator, we increased our push notifications the drivers were receiving, enabling the drivers of the vans to solve their challenges faster on their own.

This served two purposes: higher customer satisfaction and higher profitability. By recognizing and addressing the issue in real time, our customer service inquiries decreased by 10 percent. Remember the 289 cargo vans we put on the road in the first three months which led to 15,000 over the next five years? We achieved that by really leaning into managing both leading and lagging indicators and updating our strategy on a quarterly basis based on that information.

If you are not utilizing both leading and lagging indicators to inform your strategy, you're always going to be late to the game, and you're not going to be in the best position to execute a business transformation.

While management is highly focused on tasks and KPIs, at the center of it all is the managing of people. Some people may refer to this as the softer side of management, but it is also the more complex side. Setting deadlines, managing milestones, providing feedback, managing meetings, schedules, client expectations, budgets, performance reviews, and career progression are challenging people aspects of management that don't provide you a dashboard of visual metrics letting you know whether you are on the right track or you have veered off course.

Coach

Leading is not just putting a vision out in front and expecting everyone to run toward that vision at the same speed. The fact is not everyone will be able to run at the same transformative speed and some will unintentionally run in a different direction. It is the responsibility of the leader to harness the capabilities of all team members by providing them the support and resources to get them up to speed and running in the right direction. This is where coaching is key.

Simply telling people to work harder is not coaching. Coaching is about taking the time to show someone how they can be more efficient and effective in their role. It's sitting with them and saying, "Let me walk you through the steps," and periodically checking back in with them until they are confident that they can get it done. It's defining the processes better. It's holding more collaborative meetings that empower people to figure it out. It's offering time and patience to help someone do better and be better. Coaching shows people the way.

There were many opportunities to coach team members from Merchants' evolutionary process to our transformational process. Here's one example.

Once a leasing vehicle had been ordered for a client and put on the road, it went into our system as *on the road* and was subsequently billed. Every Friday, a team member would print all the leasing orders and put them on the desk of the person who would come in on Saturdays to sign them. I didn't understand the rationale for what seemed like extraneous steps in an otherwise simple process. It would have been easy for me to say, "Yeah, we're not going to do it that way anymore," tell them how I wanted them to do it, and walk away, but instead, I chose to seize the coaching opportunity before me.

Here's how the coaching conversation with the people involved with the process went.

"When we put a vehicle on the road, it's already been approved, and electronically in the system and everything is done, correct?"

"Yes."

"Then we print them and sign them?"

"Yes, so we have a signed copy."

This is where I love to use the whiteboard as a collaborative tool. I began to write out the steps to the process.

"So," I said, "once the vehicle is on the road, it's already in the system and it's being billed for, correct? I just want to re-verify this."

"Yes."

"Okay, step one is ordering the vehicle, step two is getting it on the road, step three is putting it in the system, and step four is billing for it. What's next?"

"We print it, sign it, and file it."

I added steps five, six, and seven to the list and asked, "Where do we file it? Do we ever access the file cabinet?"

"In an offsite file cabinet that is in a warehouse. And no, I can't remember ever accessing it."

"What if we need to reach the client about their lease?"

"We go into our online system where we have all the information."

"So, we never have a need to access the filed paper copy?"

"Now that I think about it, I don't know of any reason we would need to access the paper copy."

"Great. Now that we have all this information in front of us, does anyone feel like we need to continue doing steps five, six, and seven?"

By then, the answer was clear that we didn't, and we were able to assure everyone that their job was not being taken away but rather their time had been freed up for them to do more meaningful value-added work, and we brainstormed about what that might look like.

If I had simply told them to stop printing, signing, and filing and moved on, the individuals involved would not have understood the mindset shift Merchants was engaging in nor would they have understood that they had the autonomy to suggest and/or make these types of decisions in the future. I would have been *managing* those types of changes for as long as I was there. But I didn't because our team members had developed the skills and confidence to look at how to do things in new ways and collaborate with each other on how to make them more efficient and effective.

This transition is essential to any transformation, because while you, the leader, may be authoring the big changes, it is all the team members across the company who are doing the work to make the transformation happen. And if they aren't empowered to grow, be better, and transform, then your business transformation will have a self-imposed ceiling on it. If the people doing the everyday work aren't part of the transformation because leadership hasn't coached them and helped them understand how to transform and think differently, the result will be a leadership transformation, not a company transformation.

So, let me ask you an important question. If coaching is so important to transformational growth, and I would argue it's important for all strategies, then why do leaders do such a poor job of it?

The answer is simple: TIME. Coaching takes a lot of time. You must choose to invest. Ready for this? You need to slow down to go fast. Let me repeat that. For all your team members to speed up and move faster than your competitors, leaders must slow down to help them grow. I know this sounds so obvious but look at your schedule and meetings and ask yourself how often you slow down to coach junior people in your organization. I hope you answered often, but my experience tells me most people struggle with this. Once you choose to commit to being a more active coach in your company, you will love seeing people grow based on the influence you have been able to inject into them. Coaching provides me my motivational "juice."

We now know that Transformational Leadership is the willingness to accept responsibility to organize a group of people to achieve an *extraordinary* goal, and that the development of a truly transformational senior leadership team is the foundation upon which all other components of a transformation process will be built.

Now, it's time to take it a step further. For an organization to disrupt and transform, every person in the company must be embedded in the process successfully and fearlessly. For that to happen, senior leadership must establish and fuel a transformational culture.

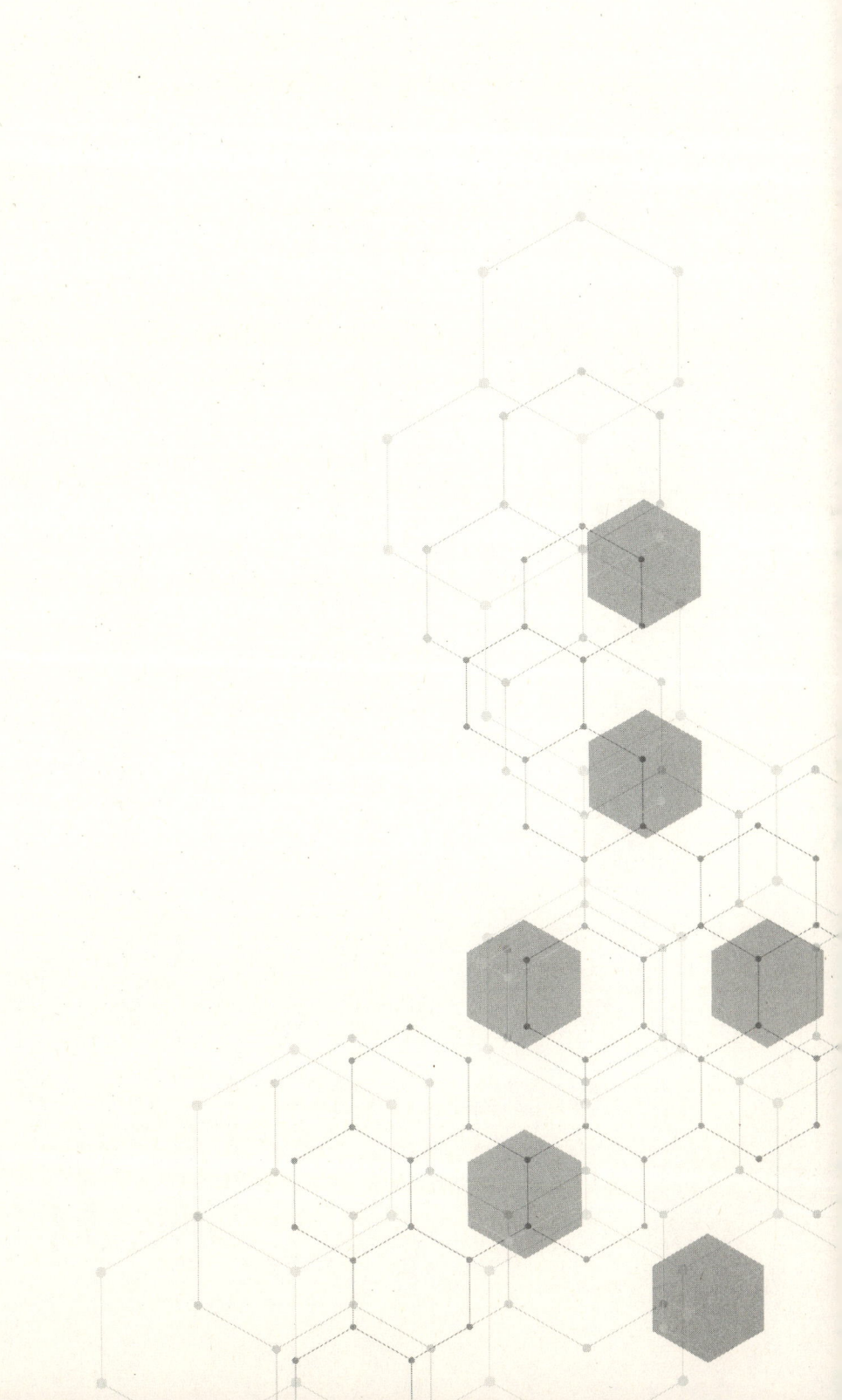

CHAPTER 4

PILLAR 2: CULTURE

As I walked through the building, not one person greeted me or even raised their eyes to look at me. No one asked me who I was, what I was doing there, or if I needed any help. People were crammed into tiny workspaces, the carpet was stained and worn, and the lights were dim. It was an environment with no energy, no heartbeat, and no comradery. This company was in a death spiral, and the board was waiting for my answer. Would I accept the position of president and CEO?

As I walked out of the first building and across campus to the next building, I called my wife Dana and gave her the update. "Dead as can be. No energy. A real opportunity here! I am going to call the board on my way to the airport later and let them know I am going to accept. I just need to check out the other buildings on campus to see if I get the same sense and vibe from the employees."

When I visited the next building, where many of the executives resided, it was more of the same. The carpet wasn't as bad and lights weren't out, but the energy had been sucked out of these people too.

As part of my interview process, ahead of entering any business trans-formation, or in this case a true turnaround, I request an unannounced visit to the company to see firsthand the true, unvarnished view of the company's culture, before I experience what I know will be the artificial A-game everyone will bring the first day the new boss arrives.

If it had been a stellar company with a great vibe, lots of col-laboration, high energy, and great synergy, there would have been nothing to turn around. But for a failing company in a declining market, there was nothing else to do but improve and transform. The truth is, if I did nothing else but run around the building every day high-fiving people and telling them we're going to kick some ass, the company would have automatically improved. That simple daily sharing of positivity would have changed the company's culture—not enough for transformative success—but it would have shifted it, because everything leaders do, or in this company's case, don't do, impacts the development of their culture.

Ever heard of the broken window theory? It's the idea that each problem (even one broken window) that is not fixed in a given envi-ronment affects people's attitude toward that environment and leads to more problems. An analogy that comes to my mind is dressing rooms. If you go to a store, and in the dressing room, clothes are left behind in mounds and piles, it makes you wonder if the clothes you brought in with you are worth trying on. After all, nobody else seemed to like what they tried on. It's also tempting to toss your clothes on the pile, rather than bring them to the front or return them to the rack. See the theory is once the windows are broken, or the pile is created, it makes it okay to break more windows and create more piles.

Now, there are stores that would never let this happen because that is not their culture. Lululemon is one of those stores. When you approach a Lululemon dressing room, you are greeted by an attendant who writes your name on the dressing room door, offers to get you different sizes or colors, and takes the clothes you are not purchasing and folds or hangs them up and puts them back for other customers to access immediately. There's no pile and no mess, sending the message that Lululemon values their products and you should too.

This is a culture set by the company but also reinforced by the physical layout, the procedures of the stores, and the training of the team members. All those aspects together play an active role in developing the culture.

Your company's culture is a living entity that you must take care to continually cultivate. If a window breaks, or in my new company's case, if a bulb goes out, replace it. Expecting people to work in small, dirty, dimly lit offices creates a culture of "Why bother?" A company cannot even stay the course with that culture: evolving or transforming would be impossible.

The company I was excited to turn around serviced computers through warranty services. In the late 1990s, these warranties were extremely valuable and as the prices of laptops and desktops (yes, there were once upon a time actual desktop computers) decreased dramatically in the early 2000s, the warranties began to become obsolete. People were no longer willing to shell out $200 to $300 for a warranty on a $900 laptop that was headed toward becoming a $600 laptop by the time they might need the warranty. The inevitable decline was obvious, but this company had chosen not to adapt to the shifting market.

That was all about to change.

As a new leader of the company, one of my first steps would be to view the company from what I call the rightSIDE up, a methodology for fixing distressed companies that I had developed over the years as a turnaround CEO. This methodology requires you to look at EVERYTHING from the right side, no matter how tempting it is to look at it from the wrong side.

For this company, the wrong side was focusing on the fact that no one was buying their warranties anymore and choosing to just keep cutting internal expenses to try and keep their heads above water for a bit longer. Cutting costs has NEVER been a winning long-term strategy.

Here's what the rightSIDE up looked like from my perspective.

- People were still buying tons of warranties, just not warranties for personal computers.
- The company had two incredible core capabilities—ten thousand technicians who could service any home or business in North America and mechanically trained technicians who could fix stuff.

With this perspective, it was clear that the company just needed to find new markets and products that could leverage these two core capabilities. Can you think of any? What equipment is more expensive than a laptop, breaks from time to time, requires mechanical skills to fix, and is in nearly every city across North America? Medical equipment, manufacturing equipment, HVAC equipment, ATMs, and more. These markets were still purchasing warranties for their products, we just needed to pivot to those markets.

I shared my rightSIDE up perspective with everyone in the company to instill confidence that there was in fact a future for this company. In the first two months, I also had all the lights and carpeting replaced—the bar had fallen so low that people thought working lights and new, clean carpets were amazing. Over the next two years, we invested in the company and our employees, providing training opportunities, employee recognition and appreciation, and appropriate compensation and benefits.

A few months after I started—it was opening day of the baseball season—our employee recognition and appreciation were in full swing. I had asked the HR team if we could have an opening-day party in which all team members could wear baseball shirts and hats, fire up some hot dog steaming machines, and have popcorn in the office and send popcorn to all our technicians around North America. The HR leader's first response was "Do you know how much work that is going to be?"

"Yes I do, but the ROI will be amazing," I said. And it was. Opening day became a pivotal day in the company's turnaround, because it was the day everyone understood that the culture was shifting. In that time, our company changed its culture from one that had employees thinking "Why bother?" to asking, "How can I be and do better?"

As the CEO, I could have knocked all the other transformation pillars out of the park, but if I hadn't changed the culture right out of the gate to one of transformation and made sure that everyone was aligned with that culture, the company may have evolved a bit, but we would not have been able to transform and achieve the level of success that we did.

Here are some leading and lagging indicators that proved just how far we had moved the needle.

In nine months, the company's employee satisfaction survey improved from 52 percent to 79 percent. That was the lagging indicator. I was thrilled that the satisfaction of the employees had increased by 27 percent, which was literally a 50 percent increase. I knew that in the years to come, we would get the score into the eighties.

Now, the percentage of employees who completed the survey also increased, jumping from 27 percent to 82 percent—a 200 percent increase! That was the leading indicator. Those numbers were great, but it was what those numbers represented that really energized me. We had captured the hearts and minds of the employees. We were winning inch by inch.

Creating a Transformational Culture

When I was with Merchants, I had a replica of a Formula 1 car installed in the lobby. With anyone who visited the company and asked the receptionist, "What's up with the car?" the receptionist would share Merchants' twelve economic engines, custom-built strategy, and culture. Now, were they able to share all the details of all of Merchants' twelve economic engines? Probably not, but they were able to name all of them and gave great details on their favorites, because everyone in the company had a clear understanding of our overall strategy and culture.

So, why did I have an F1 car installed in Merchants' lobby?

When we made the decision to kick off our business transformation, we immediately needed to distinguish ourselves from our competitors. When I moved into the role of CEO, Merchants had seven competitors in the long-term leasing arena, and we sat at number eight. As a former client and board member, I always thought it was a real challenge for a fleet company to differentiate themselves solely on long-term leasing. The analogy we used to explain this was that we were all driving modified stock cars on the same oval NASCAR racing course; a course on which drivers can only turn left. It's tough to beat your competition when you're all offering a remarkably similar value proposition that has prospects saying they are "exactly the same thing."

For Merchants to truly transform, we couldn't do it with a NASCAR stock car and oval racetrack. For Merchants to transform and disrupt the industry, we needed to build the equivalent of a Formula 1 race car and drive on a different racetrack. F1 racing machines are custom built from the ground up for high performance at every speed and every turn, and they are modified every week for every unique racetrack the circuit throws at them. Merchants needed to transform from a NASCAR car to a Formula 1 car.

Our transformational leadership was in place, and we had a strategy to provide a custom-built, high-performance race car for our clients. Now, it was time to create the culture that would shift our strategy into gear, and it was critically important to paint a picture—the race car analogy—for all our team members to understand and embrace.

It Was Time to Decide, Assess, and Plan

DECIDE what you want the culture to be. Deciding what you want your culture to be requires hard-core commitment and a high degree of transparency. You aren't deciding on a culture for the next quarter or year; you are determining the culture that will be embedded in your organization's DNA beyond the life of its leader. Your culture must align with and fuel your strategy and vision. This is not something to be taken lightly.

Imagine how well Google's culture would align with and fuel a firm of corporate tax attorneys: making their own schedule and greeting their clients at the bottom of a giant slide in the lobby. That wouldn't exactly instill the confidence and trust companies look for in their legal counsel for tax compliance. On the other hand, if Google required their employees to wear suits and ties and stick to a rigid schedule, it would stymie the creative and innovative culture that they have built their success on. In both cases, little things matter from dress code to schedules to slides in the lobby and remote work policies.

Merchants decided to disrupt the fleet industry and offer—like the drive-through in the fast-food industry decades ago—something that no one else had done before. The end goal was to develop unique F1 racetracks and the unique race cars to navigate those tracks for Merchants' client relationships and product offerings. To make that happen, Merchants' culture needed to be known by three core values: service, flexibility, and innovation. The DECISION on what we wanted Merchants' culture to be—its future state—was set.

ASSESS your current state vs. your future state. The natural inclination for people when they assess their current state vs. their future state is to believe that they are relatively close to what they want their future state to be. There are two main reasons for this. The first reason is that most people naturally think they are further along their journey to success than they really are, especially when it's a business transformation. The second reason is more primitive. If there's a big gap between current state vs. future state, a lot of change will be required, and for many of us, the idea of change creates FUD (fear, uncertainty, and doubt) and a whole lot of extra work.

When we began to talk about creating a culture that valued flexibility, innovation, and client-centric service, there were many who believed we were already providing a high level of those values. I took those beliefs for a test drive and asked, "If I want a short-term lease *and* a long-term lease, and we're a company that provides flexibility, I can just call one person to fill my needs, right?" The response was, "No, you have to call two people."

At the end of the day, while we were flexible in the variety of our product offerings, Merchants' organizational structure did not have the flexibility to offer these different services and products to all its clients in an accessible and efficient way. That is not reflective of a company whose value includes flexibility. To truly be flexible, you must be flexible across all aspects of your business, including human resources, finance, client services, technology, consulting, and more.

When people said we were innovative, I challenged the leadership team to walk up to the flip chart and write down our top five innovations over the past twelve months. No one stood up. Now, I'm not suggesting that the company was doing something wrong because they weren't innovating; I was just establishing whether Merchants' current values aligned with their actions. I pushed them harder and extended the time horizon to be over the last five years. That created a little momentum for some of the company's innovations, and each story that was told was truly innovative, but there was a common thread among them.

It wasn't the company that was being innovative, it was individuals who took the initiative to do something innovative and out of the norm to be flexible for a client. And this individual, innovative spirit was great. But while the company could hang its hat on the ability to be innovative, everyone agreed Merchants was not systemically innovative. If Merchants was to continue claiming flexibility and innovation as core values, the Merchants team needed to live and breathe it every day. Leadership needed to embed these values in its culture.

If when reviewing your company's values, it's determined one or more are not the right values for your company, that's okay. Replace them with the values that *are* right for your organization and then embed those values into your culture. We made the decision to keep flexibility and innovation as two of our core values but agreed we had some work to do to make them a reality.

Now, when I challenged the leadership team to list on that same flip chart how Merchants provided high-level service, it was a race to the chart, and everyone shared story after story of going the extra mile to get a vehicle to a client or to rescue a client in a distressed situation. It was energizing to listen to all the stories, and this process reinforced my confidence in our ability to transform.

Walking through this exercise put a spotlight on the values that were embedded in the culture—service—and the ones that needed some cultural engineering—flexibility and innovation. We needed to close those gaps.

Just as deciding what your culture will be requires hard-core honesty, commitment, and transparency, so does assessing it against your future state. You must continuously test the limits of your current state against what you want your future state to be.

PLAN actions to accelerate your future state. Once the leadership team had decided what our transformational strategy and culture would be and assessed its current state vs. our desired future state, we knew we had some work ahead of us. It was time to act, and everyone was ready.

In 2018, Merchants was eighth in North America in the commercial fleet industry with 28,000 leased units. The blueprint we created was to become seventh in the industry in seven years with 70,000 leased units. It was clear and repeatable. Everyone in the company could understand and recite seventh in industry, in seven years, with 70,000 vehicles. We developed action plans for each of our three core values that would be paramount to our success in being transformative—service, flexibility, and innovation—and committed to doing whatever it took to build our future state.

Now, how would we get there FAST?

Align, Design, Fuel, and Drive

We held a company-wide meeting to share the strategic blueprint and explain to everyone that for Merchants to go from eighth to seventh in seven years, with 70,000 vehicles, each one of us needed to elevate personally and professionally. This was a new concept for many people in the company, and to introduce it, we provided everyone with an Elev8 card (elevating from eighth to seventh—kind of cute, kind of corny, but I swear this stuff works. Why? Because it's memorable! I bet you can even remember Elev8 a little more now). On one side, they were asked to list three things they were going to do to elevate themselves professionally, and on the other side, three things they were going to do to elevate themselves personally.

There was one question I was repeatedly asked, "Why do we need to elevate ourselves personally?"

My response would be that we were not going to become seventh just by working harder or because we had a winning strategy. We were going to become seventh because we were all going to develop the capability and confidence to be our best every day so we could meet the challenges ahead. To do that, we needed everyone to be healthy and strong in and out of the office. It also involved maintaining healthy relationships with family and friends and a healthy life balance. "By each team member bringing the best version of themselves to the office every day, we will grow and succeed together. We will all become Formula 1 drivers."

I'm sure there have been drivers who had all the potential in the world to be an F1 driver but never succeeded, because there was something holding them back. Maybe it was physical fitness, mental toughness, life balance, or EQ challenges. When I study the best drivers like Michael Schumacher, Lewis Hamilton, Max Verstappen, and my personal favorite Lando Norris, it's clear that they all get it. They eat well. They sleep well. They hydrate. They manage their emotions. They have healthy relationship with team members. They aren't just incredible drivers; they put the effort in to be the total package.

When you are at your best personally, do you feel that elevation of yourself transfer to the work you do? When you are crushing it at work, do you also perform your best in personal aspects of your life? My guess is that the answer to both is "yes."

Align

The first step in cultivating the culture that would fuel Merchants' vision and strategy was to get everyone, and I do mean everyone, in the company aligned with and moving in the same strategic direction and then developing a process to *keep* everyone aligned throughout the transformation process, which could be anywhere from two to five years.

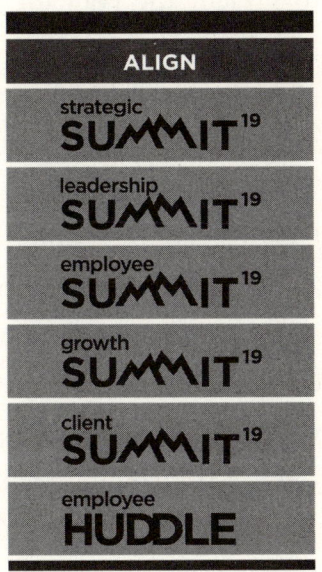

Disruptive transformation requires successes and failures, and pivots and flexibility to adjust to those successes and failures. If a company doesn't have a way to communicate and then align the team on a frequent and consistent basis, their team will not be clear on the direction, and if they aren't clear on the direction, it's impossible for them to support the direction, and without their support, it will be a challenge for a company to be successful in their market.

Company-wide alignment of vision, values, and strategic direction is critical throughout the life of the transformation.

At Merchants, the initial alignment process occurred through what became known in the company as Summit-palooza season: a series of five collaborative and strategic meetings that would align us on an annual basis followed by quarterly meetings that served as "tune-ups" and progress reports that told us how were we doing with our new F1 race car on our new track. Let's break each of these down.

Strategic Summit

Merchants' senior leadership came together at the strategic summit to present the plan for how their departments/teams would get Merchants from eighth to seventh in the industry, in seven years, with 70,000 vehicles. The first time we did this was quite the task. It was a three-day offsite event that ran from 6:00 a.m. to 10:00 p.m. each day. The leadership team had never done anything like this before, and for it to succeed, they would need to allow themselves to be vulnerable and open-minded. Anytime you bring ten different people together and put each person in a vulnerable position, you have no idea if the end results will be positive or negative. But in my experience, if you muscle through and use these settings as a "forcing mechanism," you will truly build a comradery that is special. From our senior vice president (SVP) of sales to our chief financial officer (CFO) to the head of HR, every person went through these summits and came out the other side wiser, healthier, and closer.

In fact, the leadership team dubbed themselves "besties" and had bestie bracelets made. When talking about besties, I always like to share this joke:

Do you know the difference between best friends and besties?

A best friend will help you move.

A bestie will help you move the body.

I cannot stress enough the importance of assuring that the goals of executive leadership are aligned with the strategic direction *and* with each other. Too many companies don't put the time and effort into this critical component of the process and, as a result, are unable to gain traction with their strategic direction and often, unknowingly, end up working against each other with no ill intent—they simply didn't invest enough time to truly align.

Leadership Summit

Now that the senior leadership team was in alignment, it was time to get all their direct reports in alignment, too. Our leadership summit was a two-day event in which we broke down the strategic direction and how each division was going to contribute to the Merchants' blueprint of seventh, in seven years, with 70,000 vehicles.

Marketing outlined how Merchants would go to market and build a market-leading brand. Sales outlined how Merchants would sell to prospects. Operations outlined how Merchants would deliver to what Sales had sold. Finance outlined how Merchants would fund the strategic direction and the growth of the company. HR outlined how Merchants would cultivate a great people culture and attract, retain, and develop great talent. Technology outlined how they would enable the overall strategic direction. These were not simply read-out sessions; they were working sessions. Each senior leader would listen to the specific business plan or support function of their direct reports and would contribute to the process with exercises, breakout sessions, and general input. It was a full two-day session with multiple opportunities to interact and react.

Once all our leaders were aligned, it was time to inform, educate, and align Merchants' entire workforce.

Employee Summit

The goal of the employee summit was to educate everyone on the strategic vision and *their* role in that direction. They did not need to know the same detail of information as the business and functional leaders in the company. For example, our marketing plan at the strategic summit was about one hundred pages. By the time we got to the leadership summit, it was pulled back to about fifty pages, and for the employee summit, it was further reduced to about twenty-five pages. Everyone was provided the same information, just differing amounts of detail based on their role within the company.

Now, we were ready to ignite our growth power.

Growth Summit

Once everyone in the company was aligned, we pulled all sales, marketing, and client service teams together for a two-and-a-half-day offsite meeting to reaffirm the strategic direction. We then educated them all on our new services, how we wanted them to talk about the company and its services, and how we wanted the market to perceive us. Our sales leaders trained our sales professionals on how to sell the new strategy, how to differentiate Merchants from our competition, and how we priced our deals. They also provided insights into what our competitors were doing in the marketplace.

In these meetings, we didn't talk extensively about HR, technology, or finance, but we did talk about the teams we recruited, how our technology was different than others, and how we would fund our clients' growth. To be disruptive and innovative, Merchants would need to improve year over year, which would require continuously developing new solutions. The growth summit provided the opportunity to roll out these solutions in great detail and receive feedback from our sales and marketing professionals. A benefit to each of these summits was the coming together of individuals and teams to celebrate the first steps of our transformation journey together.

Client Summit

Yes, you read that right, we even shared our strategic direction and plan for the upcoming year with our clients. This end-to-end process isn't unique to Merchants, but I think Merchants is unique in the depth and breadth with which they involve clients on an annual basis. After all, how could we expect our valued clients to help drive Merchants' disruptive growth if we weren't truly aligning and educating them on it?

We also found that by being transparent with our top clients, presenting to them everything that we presented to our leaders, employees, and sales and marketing people served to enhance our culture of service, flexibility, and innovation. By including them in the process, we had the unique opportunity to get ahead of the curve and educate our clients, but more importantly, it provided the opportunity to gain advance input from our clients so we could improve our products and services. You may be wondering, what if Merchants' clients shared our playbook with our competitors? True disruptors can't be outpaced or outplayed. Just like on the racetrack, even if the other team knows your strategy, they still need to stop you, and there was no stopping the Merchants team!

At the close of the summits, everyone from executive leadership to our clients had been educated on and aligned with our strategy to become seventh in the industry, in seven years, with 70,000 vehicles. Now, the goal was to sustain that alignment, and one of the key ways we did that was through our employee huddles.

Employee Huddles

In-person employee huddles, which occur four to six times a year, are a company-wide opportunity to reaffirm that everyone is aligned with the strategic direction, assess how we are progressing in our strategic direction, and identify if there are areas in which we are not progressing in alignment with the strategic direction and how to get those areas realigned. Huddles are a real-time training session with updates on our progress, obstacles, and new plays. In between our in-person employee huddles, we held company-wide virtual huddles once a month that functioned in the same way. And guess when we started doing these? In March 2020, when COVID hit and Zoom became a household name. This virtual connection was vital to all of us.

Finally, every Monday morning, I wrote to the company on a specific topic, from how the company was doing, to leadership lessons, to what my family and I were up to in the community and in general. You get the idea—there was a lot of investment of time being put into building a great culture by meetings, discussions, learning opportunities, and openness. If you are thinking this seems like too much, then I would warn you that a business transformation may not be right for your company, because leadership must fully commit to the future-state culture and the only way to get there is to invest the time and energy.

Without these consistent and frequent communications, it is easy for people to splinter from the direction a bit, and if those splinters are not course corrected quickly, they can create independent paths of their own. Before a company begins to implement their blueprint, they must ensure that they have the channels and cadence in place to communicate with their employees as they move through the transformation process. It is this consistent, intentional, and transparent communication up and down the ladder that will cultivate the right culture for your organization and bring the entire company along on the transformation journey.

Aligning everyone in the company with the strategic direction by building a great culture is more important than picking the right product or service to transform. Here's why. If everyone's aligned, and let's say, the new product or service that is the current focus turns out to be the wrong one, the business can fail it fast and move forward with the next potential service or product. In that same scenario, if everyone's not aligned, and the channels and cadence of communication are not in place, then the business is not equipped to quickly identify a failing product and shut it down, and the company will keep pushing the failing product or service without realizing it. And vice versa is wildly true as well, if you have a successful product launch and everyone is aligned, you can truly accelerate its path to success.

Design

Merchants' design process focused on developing the ability to innovate in ways that would disrupt the industry. We began to design the resources, communications, skills, behaviors, processes, and outcomes to enable, encourage, and inspire every team member to think innovatively. It all started with the simple decision to create an innovation department. When companies commit to an innovation department, there are usually two different ways to establish them: (1)

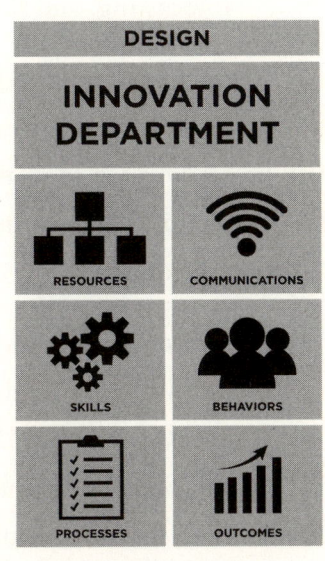

an external team that goes into the business and performs the innovation work, or (2) an internal team that trains the organization how to innovate within their teams. We chose option two. Any idea why?

Culture! We weren't looking to just establish innovation projects, we wanted to establish an innovative culture, and we believed an in-house department that would infuse the organization with the skills and know how would be more successful for Merchants. Both options work, but during a transformation, option two is more beneficial.

- *Resources* would include the development of innovation leaders and innovation coaches. At Merchants, we hired one Director of Innovation, and they trained and developed twenty innovation coaches across the entire company.
- *Communications* would include a monthly innovation email communication along with virtual meetings and a dedicated innovation hub on our intranet, SharePoint portal.
- *Skills* to be developed included design thinking, human-centered design, brainstorming, process mapping, futures forecasting, and fleetIQ.

Team members would be empowered to engage in *behaviors* that fit our service-focused, flexible, and innovative culture. They would also be empowered to challenge the status quo, think creatively, not fear failure, and engage in rapid prototyping, information sharing, and systems thinking.

- Our *processes* would be designed to facilitate and recognize the innovative spirit through INNOV8 goal setting, CELEBR8 innovations, the INNOV8R award, an innovation tracker, and SharePoint collaboration coaches.
- Our *outcomes* would be measured through client retention, client acquisition, employee engagement, employee retention, productivity, rapid testing, new offerings, and innovative technologies.

But before we could implement these designs, we needed to help people and departments overcome a "fixedness" mindset. Remember, when I came on board as CEO, we had a siloed system of seven different companies, each with a different name, a different team, and in most cases, in a different building. The fixedness we were fighting against was not only individuals who had been there for many years, but with the individual companies who were proud of their autonomy and distinct way of doing things.

During my innovation journey and as part of our learning culture, I traveled to Columbia University and took an Executive Education program on Innovation. During that weeklong program, I met Yoni Stern, a professor of the course and a consultant for SIT, an innovation company out of Tel Aviv. I was so impressed with how much I learned from Yoni that I engaged him to train Merchants' leadership team and, over time, our employees and some of our more innovative clients. Yoni taught us about our own fixedness and served as a breakthrough for us. Fixedness is a cognitive bias in which we can only see the world around us in the way we are used to seeing it. A coin for example, serves as a method of payment. A person with fixedness may not be able to see its alternate use as a screwdriver should the need arise.

Fixedness can limit our ability to creatively solve problems.

But not all fixedness is bad. It's not efficient to try to do every task in a new way. If you need to put a nail in the wall and there's a hammer handy, it wouldn't make sense to try to find another object to serve as a hammer. On the other hand, if there isn't a hammer available, fixedness could limit the person's ability to see other objects in their environment that could also drive the nail in. People, organizations, and industries can develop fixedness.

The PC company I shared with you at the beginning of this chapter had a fixed mindset that crippled them: they fixed PCs, period, and could see no other alternative. Industry fixedness kept the freezer-on-top, fridge-on-bottom structure of the refrigerator for decades beyond the technology that allowed for the many configurations of freezer/fridge compartments we see today. Know why? Because the original "iceboxes" put the ice on top, hence the freezer on top.

Through this process, we identified our areas of fixedness. One example of our fixedness was seeing short-term rental and long-term leases as separate and distinct. When I asked why we kept them separate, I was told because that's how the company was set up. "Our short-term rentals and long-term leases have different company names, different websites, they go to market differently, we have different sales teams, and two registration teams." I eased into the fixedness by asking why we couldn't have one registration team. The initial response was that the registration processes were different, but when we broke down the process for each and the desired result, it became clear that they didn't need to be different. And that is how we began to break down the fixedness mindset that had been cultivated over the course of thirty years.

Fixedness is a "safe" choice for those who are wary of taking risks and making mistakes. But "safe" won't drive transformation. Once we identified our key areas of fixedness and began to walk through alternate processes and procedures, we had to address the FUD that could hold us all back. That meant, I had to not just give permission to fail but I had to encourage it.

I told the team that if we're going to run fast, we're going to make mistakes, and mistakes were okay. In fact, we would learn more from our failures than our successes. Running fast meant we wouldn't have a spreadsheet detailing every single cost and every potential problem for every action we chose to take. We were building a culture focused on service, flexibility, and innovation that would enable us to transform Merchants and disrupt the industry, and that required taking risks. Now, don't interpret this as reckless; we were a for-profit business and although we wanted to transform, making money was part of our success.

Our design process was also iterative and always being updated, changed, and tweaked.

Fuel

The next step in the innovation process and building an innovation culture was how we were going to fuel our culture. We believed there were four key levels:

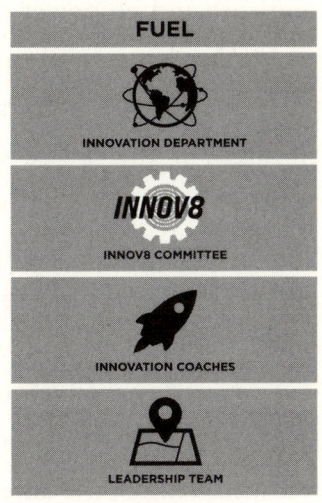

1. Leadership team to drive the innovation strategy.
2. Innovation coaches: We selected a total of twenty team members who would be trained to be innovation coaches. They would be trained in design thinking, process improvement, and my favorite, to always ask this simple question in team meetings: "Why?" Followed by, "Why not?" Upon completion of their innovation training, each coach would be embedded within the organization.
3. Innovation committee: This committee would comprise over fifty volunteers across the company along with members of our HR team. Their purpose would be to inject energy into the company and culture around change, change management, and successes. Remember when I talked about storytelling? These were our storytellers.
4. All Employees: We made the decision that everyone needed to participate in the innovation that would take place at

Merchants. More on this in the next chapter when we talk about our people.

Drive

To drive our innovative culture, we designed our innovation program to motivate and empower every member of the Merchants team to think innovatively. We provided innovation coaching throughout the entire company. We taught what innovation was and developed what we called Big I's and Small i's—big innovations and small innovations.

One of our big innovations was going into the last mile market that I discussed in chapter 3; another was collapsing all the different companies and brands into one. These were significant innovations that required agreement and alignment up and down the ladder in order to move forward. The Small i's were the ones that would determine if our transformation would be successful in the long term.

My favorite Small i's of all time came from one of our auto service technicians. Recruiting and keeping technicians can be challenging, and he had an idea to help with recruitment. He did oil changes all day long and he thought, "What if we put a recruitment sticker on the oil filter, so when our clients pull into a Jiffy Lube or Valvoline to have their vehicle serviced, the technician will see it?" He had the idea for simple taglines like, "Do you have 401(k) benefits? You will if you join the Merchants team," or "Do you have full health coverage? You will if you join the Merchants team."

When our team member brought that idea to us, we were almost two years into our transformation, and that's when I knew our innovative culture had really taken root. It's easy for a new CEO, an executive team, or a director of innovation to believe they have an innovative culture based on a few successful innovations. But the real proof is when individual contributors at every level take advantage of the training and empowerment offered and act on it. Now, that doesn't mean everyone will act on it. What it does mean is that you've given everybody the opportunity to participate.

To wrap up the culture chapter, let me walk you through one more powerful example of bringing values to life so that people can "feel" them. Merchants needed the values that drove its culture to be integrated into every aspect of the business, including the design of our physical space.

We determined early on that to truly align our culture, we needed to all come together, not just as one company, but under one roof. For that to happen, we needed to reside in one building. We called the design and building of our new headquarters Project One. In our first meeting with the architect we said, "When people walk through the door, we want them to say service, flexibility, and innovation." Throughout the architectural process, we would describe what we wanted the feeling to be. This direction and the architect's understanding of the culture we wanted our building to reflect is what prompted more workspaces that inspired collaboration and innovation. Even the architect wanted every person who worked on our new building to know what the "vibe" should be (he wrote "service, flexibility, and innovation" on every blueprint), and his dedication to our vision is seen throughout Merchants' headquarters.

Once the right transformational leadership is driving the right transformational culture, it's time to jump into attracting, developing, and retaining the right transformational PEOPLE.

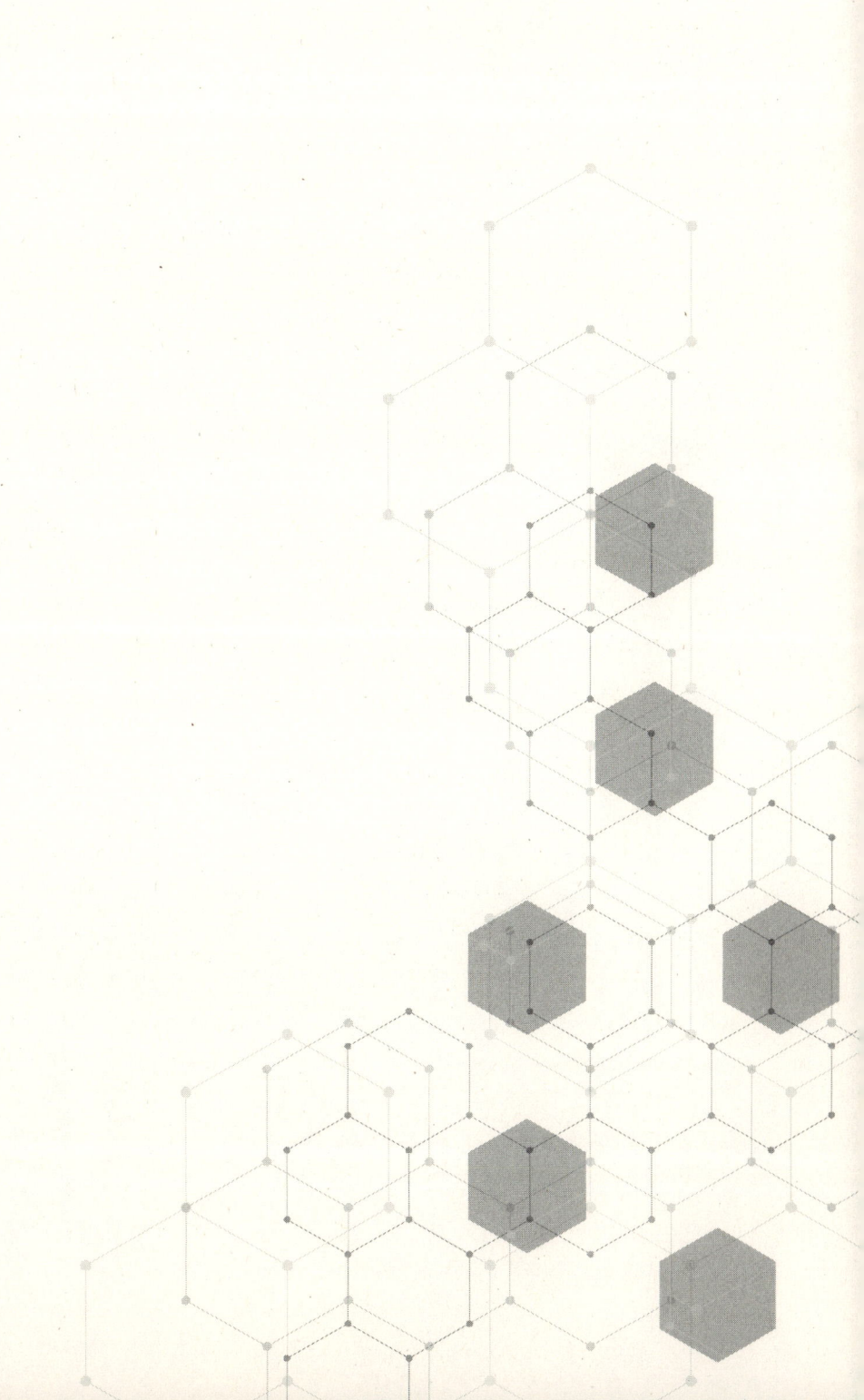

CHAPTER 5

PILLAR 3: PEOPLE

A few times a year, I receive an "alumni update" from my high school about student and faculty accomplishments and cool things happening for the Bishop Guertin Cardinals. About a decade ago, I noticed a new "tagline" for the school: Known. Valued. Treasured. After a few years of seeing the tagline appear at the bottom of the newsletter and knowing parents of current students, I asked, "What does 'Known. Valued. Treasured.' mean?" And then the infomercials began! Every parent I asked launched into a highly spirited, sometimes emotional, commentary that went something like this:

Every student at the school has their own identity and is known by the teachers. The contributions of every student are valued, and every student is treasured by the school, teachers, coaches, and administrators.

Impressive. After hearing this over and over, I asked a few students I had coached in youth sports the same question. And boom, the informercial continued. "I really like BG because being a good student is valued," said one former youth football player. "I am not a sports person, but I like to fish so we started a bass fishing team," said another. "I really like the vibe at BG and that I can choose my own path," said a third student.

This small high school in Nashua, New Hampshire, had imprinted the importance of people in their culture and in their community. Like any other high school, they had "school values" supported by programs, students, parents, and various associations. I was so intrigued by their focus on people, that I started to form a new relationship with the school. I went from being a happy but passive alum to an active one. I didn't have any kids at the school nor were my kids going to attend BG, but I was so impressed by the importance the school administration put on people that I was drawn in. With a strong leadership foundation, supported by an amazing culture, investing in people comes naturally.

Or does it?

The Right Culture Only Works If It's Filled with the Right People

In the last chapter, I shared that one of Merchants' express lube technicians came up with the idea to put a recruitment sticker on the oil filter as an example of how embedded our innovation culture had become. I reference it again now to hit home that when I talk about people for your transformation, I'm talking about every single person in your organization. While the right leadership is vital to a transformation, it is only one component. Everyone in your organization must participate in driving your transformational culture. We're talking about your receptionist, your oil change technician, your technical people, your help desk people, your directors, your vice presidents, and your senior leadership.

We're talking about creating the *wave*.

The further down the organization that you see people standing up and demonstrating that they are all in, the more successful your transformation will be, because people expect a senior VP to be on board with the transformation. They have the authority, responsibility, and the skills to make it happen. But when team members see the individual managers and individual associates demonstrating the transformation culture and pulling their peers onto the transformation train—when you see that shift begin to happen—you know everyone in the organization is going to participate in the inevitable wave that will hit their department, area, and desk.

You know the wave I'm talking about. Even if you haven't participated in one, I'm guessing you've seen it when watching a stadium event. Like the shift that takes place in a transformation, not everyone participates in the wave the first time around. One person or a group of people will begin. They stand, raise up their arms, and sit down again while urging the person next to them to do the same. That first time around, they might get a group in their section to join, but as they watch the rest of the stadium, they'll see only a smattering of people stand and wave until it peters out before it makes it halfway around. But they don't give up. They put more effort into rallying the people in their section to join in, and then they start another round. This time, there are bigger groups of people participating, and the smatterings of people standing and waving make it almost three-quarters of the way around the stadium.

The original wavers see that their actions are starting to make an impact, and they begin a third wave, and as they do so, they cheer louder and stomp their feet harder to get people excited to join in. Their excitement becomes contagious, and some of the people who stood in the last round are no longer standing because the person next to them nudged them to do it, but because they don't want to miss out. They are now putting down their popcorn and drink and watching the wave instead of the game, because they want to be ready when their turn comes. Their increased enthusiasm gets the people around them to stand and wave for the first time.

With each round, more people join in, and the pace of the wave picks up steam. The excitement builds so much that by the last round even the curmudgeons who have resisted the other six or ten rounds, say, "Fine," and join in. When the whole stadium is cheering and stomping and standing and waving their arms in the air, it's electrifying. And when people sit back down after the final round, everyone is smiling and laughing at the strangers around them, because they've all been connected by something bigger than themselves.

It's powerful stuff. And like the wave, it is the people in your organization who will bring each other along the transformational journey. Leadership may start it, but it's the people who carry the wave around the full stadium.

How do you create those waves? By getting the right people.

Who Are the Right People for Your Transformation?

In determining who the right people are for your transformation, you will need to assess both the attributes and skills necessary for successful execution of your vision. Once you know what attributes and skills are necessary, you'll assess the gaps between the current state of the attributes and skills of your people and your desired state of the attributes and skills required for your transformation. Let's begin with assessing for attributes.

Attribute Assessment

One of the key attributes required for transformation is intellectual curiosity. Intellectual curiosity is the desire to learn more about the world around us. Those who are intellectually curious actively seek out and engage in new information by asking "why" and "how" with purpose. The great news is, intellectual curiosity can be developed, and it is incumbent upon leadership to help individuals do so by cultivating a culture that encourages, empowers, and models that type of open wonder without judgment.

If no one is asking, "Why don't you think that will work?" or "How do you think we might make this work better?" there will be no new ideas, no innovation, and no transformation.

Other attributes that go hand-in-hand with transformation are creativity, open-mindedness, and the ability to handle change and lead change management. With any transformation comes significant change. While not everyone will be excited about making changes—in fact most people won't be—you must have people who can handle change and change management and be ready, willing, and able to change, even if they don't enjoy it.

And can you take a guess at the top two most important aspects of change management? Don't get all academic on me or think too big. Just think about changes you have been through. What did you value the most?

I bet it was transparency and education. You wanted to know what the change was, why it was happening, and you wanted to know the real reasons (no corporate-speak), even if not pleasant. You also wanted to learn more about the change, how it would benefit the company, where it would lead you to and why.

This reminds me of two change management experiences in my career that were managed in drastically different ways.

The first experience occurred in 1998 when the company announced an employee layoff. The memo we got from corporate talked about how much they valued their employees, how well the company was doing, and how much they regretted "right sizing" the company. What the heck is right sizing? I wondered. And if the company was doing so well, why were layoffs happening and how did that show they valued us? I still remember popping into a friend's office and asking them, "Do you fully understand what this memo means?" It turns out the layoffs were needed and warranted but sugarcoating the message—not being transparent or educational—created a negative impact.

My second change management experience was in 2006 and was so much better. An all-hands employee town hall meeting via conference call was held where they announced that the company had been struggling the past few quarters and it was time to make some tough decisions. They had to lay off 5 percent of the employee base, but they assured us they did not expect to have to do this again. The leadership also announced that they would follow up with monthly town halls for the next six months to outline the plan forward—and they did. The key differences in the second change management that significantly improved the experience:

- verbal meeting instead of memo
- direct, transparent communication
- follow-up educational meetings for the next six months

Two similar situations, two different approaches, and two wildly different receptions by the employees.

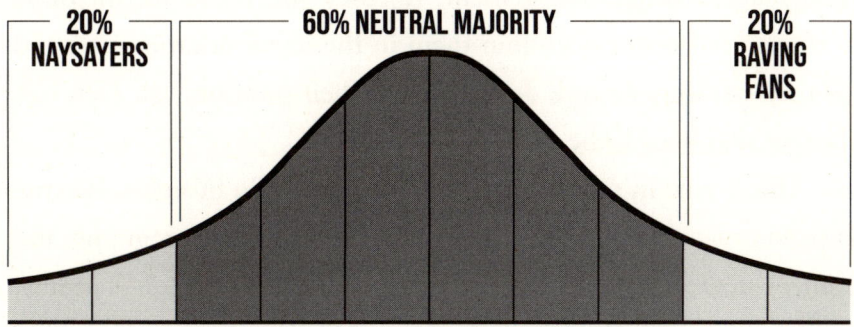

That brings us back to the bell curve from chapter 2. You will never get 100 percent of your people to change. You'll initially get about 20 percent who embrace the changes you put before them and are ready to go. These are your raving fans—your wave igniters, and you want to leverage their "let's go" spirit to help inspire the 60 percent neutral majority to stand up and wave alongside them.

The neutral majority aren't necessarily unwilling, but they do require more clarity on the destination or more information on how they will get there or how they will benefit. It will take time and effort to get them to decide. Remember, they want to be educated on why they should become a raving fan.

Finally, you have 20 percent naysayers. The "I'm not doing that" or "That's not possible" people. Now, some of these naysayers will be your best performers, but that doesn't mean they're your transformationalists, because they often operate with the fixed mindset that I talked about in chapter 4. The "I know what I'm doing, I've been doing it a long time, and I don't see reason for me to do it differently" mindset.

These are the people you must remove from the organization—voluntarily or involuntarily—as quickly as possible. Why? Because

(1) they lack the necessary transformational attributes of intellectual curiosity, creativity, open-mindedness, and the ability to handle change and change management; (2) they will try to recruit those in the neutral majority to join them in the naysayer's minority; and (3) they can impede and, depending on their position, can even halt changes that need to be made.

This is true in many aspects of life, not just in business. It's true in parent teacher organizations (PTOs), youth soccer programs, and homeowners' associations. Think about it. When someone's against something, what's the first thing they do? They recruit allies. "Do we want dogs in our condo association? No, we don't. Come to the meeting Thursday, so we can vote against it." Unfortunately, this negative strategy can be more effective than a positive one. Studies have shown that a negative connection has a greater impact than a positive one—as much as four to seven times greater![8] As a transformational leader, it is important you recognize and understand this.

Let's think political ads, and even though we hate them, guess what works—going negative. And although I absolutely hate that negativity has such pull, as a leader embracing a transformation, you must realize this and meet the naysayers head on.

The more dangerous naysayers are the silent ones—I call them the silent assassins. These are the parents who sit quietly on the sidelines game after game, never interacting with the coach or asking questions until the board meeting. That's when they show up with a list of complaints about how the team is being managed, catching everyone off guard. Dangerous in that they don't let the coach know their feelings so something productive can be done about it.

---

8   Shilagh Mirgain, "How others influence your happiness," May 25, 2019, https://www. uwhealth.org/news/the-happiness-ripple-effect.

When you have a team member, especially one who is in a leadership position, who is quietly sitting on the sidelines, who is going along to get along, who by all outward appearances is "on board" with the transition, and then you find out a month or two later that they have not, in fact, implemented all the changes they led you to believe they had—the damage has already been done.

While some naysayers may eventually be capable of and willing to make the necessary changes, they are not the people you want to expend too much time and effort on. You want to concentrate your time and effort on your raving fans: the people who are willing to embrace change and try new things even if they might fail. They are the ones who will generate more raving fans.

Every company has its own bell curve, and when you start a transformation, you likely won't have 20 percent who are raving fans—you might have 5 or 10 percent, maybe it's only two people. That's okay, you must start somewhere. Your job is to keep recruiting people internally and externally who have the right attributes and the right skill or the ability to develop the right skills.

Skills Assessment

The necessary attributes are the same for every transformation. The necessary skills, on the other hand, will be different for every transformation. In chapter 2, I shared my first experience as a turnaround CEO transforming an e-commerce and online catalog company into a vastly different business as a process outsourcing company. In its original iteration as a backend e-commerce structure, it required significant manual labor primarily in terms of warehouse and inventory management skills. Our transformation to a process outsourcing company meant we no longer maintained inventory, which meant we also no longer required a warehouse and all that goes with it.

Forklift driving and inventory management were existing skills of many of our employees that were no longer needed. It is in these moments that assessing the existing skills against the required transformation skills is critical. The goal is not to simply replace everyone who doesn't "fit" the new structure. The goal is to determine who the ready, willing, and able are and assess if they can upskill with support to what the organization now needs.

Fortunately, in my e-commerce scenario, we were able to redeploy about 80 percent of our people into new positions. The people skilled at inventory management were able to transfer their existing skills and develop new ones to be part of the new technology programs our transformation required. Many of the people who worked well in the warehouse were able to transfer their skills and develop new ones to help transition into our new customer service roles. This upskilling of existing employees takes commitment from the organization and its leadership. More on that in a bit.

There will always be people who simply don't have the ability to develop the necessary skills needed to cross the chasm of an organization's transformation. Accept it, because if you try to redeploy everybody when their skills don't match, it will not work for you or them.

For Merchants' transformation, we required people to lean into technology. This was a drastic change in skill sets for a company whose processes were highly manual *and* were separate and distinct for each division of the company. These processes worked extremely well for Merchants for almost sixty years, but they would not enable transformational growth.

Let me tell you about the Blue Folder.

The now-famous Blue Folder contained all the titles, leases, and registrations critical to the company. As the company had expanded over the past sixty years, it had spread out into multiple buildings within walking distance of each other. During one period of expansion, they acquired an old cigar store, during another, it was an old Chinese restaurant, and yet another found them purchasing a residential home to fill their growing needs. Just as every division within the company functioned distinctly different from each other, so too were each of the structures that housed them.

Every day, sometimes multiple times a day, the Blue Folder would be walked from building to building to building. One of these building-to-building transports was across a busy street, and the joke was who was going to play Frogger today and run across the street dodging traffic to get the Blue Folder where it needed to be. The company's risk manager was not a fan of this Frogger game!

The Blue Folder held the only copies of these critical documents, and I remember one day hearing the receptionist ask over the intercom, "Has anyone seen Michigan? Title number 7, 2, 8, 4. It has fallen out of a Blue Folder."

When I asked, "Why do we do that?" the answer was, "We've always done it that way." And yes, in 2018, we still had an intercom in a professional office, and we also had pink tile bathrooms, but that's all the fun part of a transformation.

That's fixedness right there, but there was also pride in the fact that they did what they needed to do to get the job done, even if that meant an occasional real-life game of Frogger. Our clients would often say that nobody worked harder than Merchants—and when I was a client, I felt the same way. I truly admired the dedication of the Merchants team and told them they should be proud of that dedication and how hard they worked to get the job done. I then explained that when things get done differently every time at every location and it's purely out of hard work that we succeed, we cannot scale the business.

Yes, our current smaller clients were happy with our current level of service, but we wouldn't be able to do business with bigger-volume clients if we didn't automate our systems. In other words, if we wanted to "Stay the Course" we were doing awesome and did not need to change. Frogger could remain in place and so could the Blue Folder. But if we wanted to transform and do business with the who's who in the world, we needed to build scalable and tech-enabled systems.

While we will talk about systems in depth in the next chapter, I mention it here, because systems are intricately connected to the people. Just as culture can't be discussed without also talking about leadership and people, the necessary attributes and skills of the people who will transform your business can't be discussed without talking about the systems they will be asked to operate and work within.

Every one of the eight pillars for transformational growth—Leadership, Culture, People, Systems, IQ, EQ, Flexibility, and Fearlessness—is interconnected and an essential component of a successful transformation.

Filling the Gaps

Automating processes like the Blue Folder would require filling both the attribute gaps and the skill gaps. The attribute gaps would be filled with a mindset shift from fixedness to open-mindedness and from FUD to fearlessness. Our shift away from fixedness began with our training with Yoni Stern, the professor from Columbia University that I told you about in chapter 4.

That fixedness training would serve as our springboard into innovation, and Merchants' new Align, Design, Fuel, and Drive blueprint (also discussed in chapter 4) would ensure that our new, innovative mindset would be embedded in our culture.

Now, the courage to overcome the FUD that can result from fixedness—after all, if you've always been directed to and rewarded for doing something one way all the time, it can be a little scary to even suggest a new way of doing things, let alone actually do it that way—would have to be built on trust. That meant we would need to give people the autonomy and confidence to make decisions and the permission to fail, or as I like to say, give them *the courage to fail and the faith to succeed.*

When we first began to encourage autonomy and those first mistakes happened, we didn't take away anyone's autonomy to make future decisions, we coached them through what happened and how they could do it better next time. We helped them develop their skill and their confidence. This happened throughout every facet of the organization.

One example was in customer service. When one of our customers arrived to pick up a vehicle they thought they were renting for that week and found out it wouldn't be ready until the following week, they complained to the customer service rep that they lost business because of the delay.

Pre-mindset shift, the customer service rep's response would have been to apologize to the customer for the inconvenience and let them know they would speak to their manager to see how they could make it right. This might take a couple of days as the question went up and then back down the chain of command while the customer service rep waited for direction.

With our new empowered and innovative mindset, the customer service rep apologized for the inconvenience and waived their fee for their first month's rental. The problem did not take forty-eight hours to resolve—it was resolved in that moment. The customer walked away feeling heard and satisfied. You know who else felt good about the exchange? Our customer service rep who had the autonomy to solve the problem for the customer on the spot.

In this instance, the rep's resolution was too great for the problem it was resolving—a free week vs. a month. That's where coaching came in. Their manager sat down with them and said, "Let's walk through what happened before you made the decision. Did you consider what your options were?" Remember when I talked about patience when coaching, this was a great teaching moment.

The employee admitted that they didn't really think about it, a month just seemed like a good idea. "That's okay," said their manager. "Now that you've had time to think about it, what do you think all your options were?" They talked through the dilemma and the employee now understood why one free week made more sense. The teaching moment doesn't end there, because every problem will be different, and the employee needed to learn how to navigate each of them.

The manager went on to acknowledge that it can be difficult to make an immediate decision with the customer right in front of them and then coached the rep on techniques to manage that. Together, they agreed that it would be okay for the rep to say to the customer, "If you could please wait here a couple of minutes, I'll go see what I can do." Then, walk around the corner, take a breath, and think through the options before offering one to the customer. Our employee now had the autonomy to make *a* decision and the tools to make the *right* decision. In this scenario, coaching was the key that built the trust necessary for that team member to overcome their FUD.

People will make mistakes, but I will take all those mistakes and inexperience over being paralyzed by fear of failure every day. If you want to move your company forward, you must empower your people to make competent decisions. If you want to retain good people, you must empower them to make competent decisions. The way to do that is let them know that it's okay to try and fail sometimes, and then coach them through the experience to help them learn, improve, and grow.

Now Let's Talk About Filling the Skills Gap

A person can ooze all the essential attributes, but if those attributes aren't paired with the right skill set, they won't be equipped to get the job done. If you set expectations for your employees, you must provide them with the training and development necessary to meet those expectations. To that end, you must first ensure that everybody in the company understands their role and contribution to the transformation and how they will be supported in fulfilling them.

This upskilling of existing employees takes commitment from the organization and its leadership. At Merchants, we had a program called LearnIQ which is a micro-credential program available to all Merchants employees at an extensive list of universities. And everyone in the company is encouraged to enroll in courses throughout the year. We have curated programs to meet specific roles in the company. This is incredibly helpful when someone is preparing to move into a new role, and the training content they need to upskill is all laid out and accessible to them.

Learning and training must be continuous for everyone, not just in preparation for a change in responsibilities. As part of every employee's annual review at Merchants, they discuss with their manager goals for the upcoming year, not just company-related goals but in areas where the employee has an interest in expanding their knowledge base. That learning may be through LinkedIn or other avenues the employee has explored. This expectation increases skills but also shifts mindsets from "how do I just get by in my job?" to "how do I want to improve myself?"

This type of training goes hand-in-hand with providing coaching throughout the person's transition as well as leadership's responsibility to role model continuous learning and growth. As CEO, it was imperative that my team saw that I was invested in continuous learning. As marketing began to play a bigger role at Merchants, I enrolled in a digital marketing course at the Wharton School of the University of Pennsylvania. I had never had a marketing role, and if I was going to bring my A-game, I needed to upskill in that area.

I think I have hit home that transformation involves drastic change. I love change, and so I have a greater capacity for it than most. To lead those who do not view change in the same way I do, I needed to know how to help them through it. To do that, I needed to upskill my understanding of how change impacts people and what their endurance level for change might be. So, I enrolled in a neuroscience course at Massachusetts Institute of Technology (MIT). I learned a tremendous amount in that course, but my biggest takeaway was that I needed my team to focus on better sleep. We had a lot of hard-charging people, and good health—in particular, good sleep—was key to one's ability to endure change. It became part of the conversation, and that's when I began handing out Fitbits to encourage people to be mindful of their sleep patterns. The knowledge I obtained inspired me to be more intentional about recognizing whole person health by addressing who people are in and out of the office.

One approach to acknowledging and encouraging whole person health was through Merchants' Elev8 cards that I shared with you in chapter 4. We introduced the Elev8 cards at the beginning of

Merchants' transformation and incorporated them annually. At the start of each year, everyone in the company was asked what one thing they were going to do over the next twelve months to elevate themselves professionally. For some that was learning Excel, for others, it involved becoming more confident with presenting to a group. Everyone was also asked what one thing they were going to do to elevate themselves personally. I remember when we rolled that out the very first time, not everyone was comfortable sharing. I told them they didn't have to fill out their personal Elev8 card if they didn't want to, and then, I thought maybe a picture on the wall would be helpful. So, right outside my office, we have what we initially called the Elev8 Wall and now call the Endurance Wall.

The top of the Endurance Wall says, *What are you going to do to drive your endurance professionally and personally?* People answer the question on sticky notes and stick them on the wall. The answers range from taking a LearnIQ program to running a 5k to eating better to scheduling their first colonoscopy—yup, it can get that personal. That's okay, because we want people to feel comfortable enough to share their path to becoming their best selves.

The message we were sending was that our employees were more than workers to us. That we really cared about them as a whole person, not just what they could do for Merchants. I often heard from team members how great the wall was, but one year, I received a letter from the wife of one of our employees. It was a thank-you letter for Merchants' employee wellness program. She was thankful because the program had provided her husband, after years of struggling on his own, with the support he needed to finally adopt a healthy lifestyle. She shared the positive impact his personal elevation had on their whole family.

I remember sitting in my office reading it and realizing that Merchants' culture isn't about commercial fleet; it's about changing lives.

Elevating the individual elevates the whole.

It's Time to Level Up

Just as we had asked our employees to elevate themselves, as a company we had to continually and intentionally level up to the evolving workplace, and there is nothing like a pandemic to drive this point home.

Like many businesses, when COVID hit, we began embracing remote work even though it was not the best fit for our culture. Remote work makes it challenging to keep your people trained, inspired, and living the transformation, because so many of those magical moments in a transformation are spontaneous, and you can't create genuine spontaneous connections if everything is operating through scheduled Zoom calls. But that was the reality we, and every other business, were living in, and we needed to level up to meet that reality.

During that time, we continued to value the whole person and not just the worker. Our initial Zoom calls were often far more personal than professional. We all genuinely wanted to know how everyone was faring with kids home from school, loved ones being sick, and the general feeling of isolation and fear. During that period, we would have over 90 percent attendance on our Friday Zoom calls.

We did everything we could to continue cultivating and nourishing our culture and our people during this challenging time, and we succeeded. Our employee satisfaction survey went out in the fall of 2020. I remember sitting with the head of HR in her office asking what she thought the results would come in as. Neither of us had a clue, we just knew that we had done our best. And it turned out that our best netted us an employee satisfaction score of 91 percent! Our best score ever!

We reached 91 percent because of the efforts of many, but it wouldn't have happened without the right person leading HR. When I came on board, Merchants had a positive culture. Their employee satisfaction score was a solid 74 percent—the national average is 51 percent. When I sat down with the HR director at the time, and I said, "Let's get it to 90," his response was, "We can't get it to 90." I knew then he wasn't the right transformational leader. Now, one of his direct reports said, "We can get it to 90." And she's the one who led us to scores of 89, 91, and 90 over the last three years. For the strategic role of human resources, it was easy to choose attributes over experience!

It truly is about having the right people in the right seat to lead and drive the right culture.

We had established a transformational senior leadership team that served as the foundation on which we built our culture, and that culture enabled us to attract, develop, and retain the best people. We were now ready to build the transformational system in which we would operate.

CHAPTER 6

PILLAR 4: SYSTEMS

We all know about systems—educational systems, communications systems, computer operating systems, and even our very own solar system. Systems are essential to almost everything we do, and every organization must develop the systems that are right for them. But the right system only works well if the right people are working the system.

One of my favorite stories about systems and people is the San Francisco 49ers and the NFL's Mr. Irrelevant in 2022. Each year, the last player chosen in the NFL draft pick is dubbed, "Mr. Irrelevant." That honor was bestowed on Brock Purdy when he was the 262nd and final pick in 2022.

Purdy joined the 49ers for the 2022 season as a third-string quarterback (QB) behind Trey Lance and Jimmy Garoppolo. Now, keep in mind, the previous year the 49ers traded three future first-round picks to move up to pick Trey Lance at number three. That is a huge amount of draft capital, not to mention Lance was picked 259 players ahead of Mr. Irrelevant. That same season, both Garoppolo and Lance suffered injuries that took them off the field. Mr. Irrelevant was suddenly the starting quarterback for the 49ers, and everyone expected the season to be over.

Instead, Purdy beat the GOAT (Greatest of All Time), Tom Brady, in his first start and went on to go 6-0 in his first six starts. Brock and the 49ers won the NFC West title, Jimmy Garoppolo was traded to the Las Vegas Raiders, and Trey Lance became a trivia question of greatest quarterback busts of all time after he was traded to the Dallas Cowboys and never heard from again. And one year later, Brock had the 49ers back in the Super Bowl and, as of the writing of this book, is up for league Most Valuable Player.

With any situation like this, there is speculation about how and why a Mr. Irrelevant, who is also a rookie, has managed to perform like an all-pro veteran. Is he simply an incredible athlete who was flying below the radar or did the 49ers' system enable a strong athlete to elevate beyond his skill level? I'm going with the 49ers' system. In fact, many people won't give Brock his proper due and call him a "system quarterback." The same had been said about the GOAT who was drafted in the sixth round at number 199.

The 49ers have developed an offensive system in which a good player can perform beyond their skill level—*if* the player chooses to work the system and become a great player. Brock Purdy has done a fantastic job leveraging the 49ers system to improve his performance—he is the right QB playing within the right system with the right people and that right combination won his team a spot in Super Bowl LVIII!

Now, there is absolutely no doubt that both Garoppolo and Lance had more skills, more athleticism, and more capabilities than Brock did, but for whatever reason, they did not fit the system or embrace the system as well as Purdy did. And what's wrong with being a system quarterback who wins? Wouldn't you rather be called a system quarterback, which is meant to be a slight, and be in the Super Bowl and winning Most Valuable Player (MVP) votes vs. having all the capabilities and athleticism but end up being traded and having to watch the Super Bowl from your living room? I know I would.

We've talked about the need for the right leadership, the right culture, and the right people—people who will leverage the system to improve their personal and professional game. Now let's talk about how to build the right system.

Building the Right System

Remember when I talked about last mile in chapter 3 on leadership? Well, before we built the transformational leadership team that enabled the manager who had been with Merchants for thirty years to say, "Yeah, let's jump into last mile!" the response from the non-transformational leadership that was at the helm in 2016 when I first broached the subject as a member of Merchants' board, went something like this:

Me: Wow, Merchants built this incredible system for short-term rentals for summer camps. I was wondering why summer camps.

Leadership: It's what we've been doing for thirty years.

Me: That's great. If you got every summer camp in the country to sign up for short-term rentals, how many vans would you have out there?

Leadership: We could have 3,000 vans out there.

Me: Not bad. There's this market called last mile delivery, and every September through December, they need over 100,000 cargo vans for holiday shopping for Q4—just think of all the FedEx, UPS, DHL,

129

and Amazon vans running around, and those are just the top ones. I think it's an opportunity to take what you have learned from summer camp and extend into a much bigger market like last mile.

Leadership: We do passenger vans in the summer; we can't do cargo vans in the fall with the seats, and we don't know anything about any of those big companies and the last mile delivery market.

And that was the end of the discussion even though I brought it up in every subsequent board meeting in 2017 as well. When you read that conversation, it may sound a bit far-fetched, but that was the fixed mindset of the company at that time. I have found that to be the general thinking of over 80 percent of companies that I have interacted with over my career. Are you part of that 80 percent?

Fast-forward to October 2018 when our transformation was taking root, we were building the right people and culture, and we had the right leaders in place. Merchants was ready to leverage our current system of short-term summer camp rentals to scale for what would become our wildly successful new growth engine: last mile.

When we began to look at how to scale our existing systems, we knew next to nothing about the logistics of a last mile operation. We needed to tap the brakes and think through our existing system.

We knew how to:

- Acquire vans (this time cargo instead of passenger) at a great price
- Register vans

- Transport vans to any zip code across the country to include 1,500 summer camps
- Maintain vans while in use
- Transport vans back to base for resale or rental to other clients
- Invoice and collect payment

We had an incredibly efficient and successful system already in place for camps, we just needed to apply it to a new and significantly larger market. It was time to assess the necessary parts of our system and how they would interact with each other. We began to strategize about locations for our transport and maintenance hubs—we needed ready fleets wherever our clients were. We also needed rates and payment structures and tech enablement tools, skills, and processes. I'm a technical engineer by trade, so systems building is something that's near and dear to my heart, and as such, I know the importance of building the right system and refining it as you go along.

If an organization doesn't have the right system in place, they risk relying on individual heroics to make it happen. Let me tell you, getting those initial 289 units on the road in the last quarter of 2018 did require a bit of team heroics. We were stretching our system's muscles in new ways, and it was painful at times. But as we kept working it and learning from it, our system became better and stronger. We learned when and who we needed to hire for our system to run on all cylinders. Merchants' 2018 last mile business launch was a blend of pure entrepreneurial spirit and muscles to envision and build the transformational systems that would enable Merchants to scale the business in 2019 and beyond.

Building the Right Transformational System

Not every system is built for transformation. As we discovered in chapter 2, there are three growth strategies: stay the course, evolve, and transform. Companies employing a stay-the-course or evolutionary growth strategy don't require systems that are built to scale to 30, 40, or 50 percent growth.

Once Merchants decided to move from an evolve growth strategy to a transform growth strategy, we needed to create a new blueprint for our transformation system that was broken down into four components: Strategic Direction, Leadership Foundation, Growth Engine, and Operational Machine. Here's what that looked like.

⚙ STRATEGIC DIRECTION			
VISION	MISSION	VALUES	GOALS

👤 LEADERSHIP FOUNDATION	
TALENT ACQUISITION & DEVELOPMENT	HIGH PERFORMANCE CULTURE

☑ GROWTH ENGINE		
BRAND EQUITY	SALES	NEW ENGINES

📊 OPERATIONAL MACHINE			
PEOPLE	PROCESS	TECHNOLOGY	SCALABILITY

Strategic Direction

Strategic direction is like the GPS for organizations, plotting the course for long-term success. It's not just about setting goals but creating a roadmap that guides every move and decision. Formulating a strategic direction begins with defining the organization's purpose—vision, mission, and values—and identifying its strengths and weaknesses. Built upon the foundation of that purpose, the strategic direction ensures all resources, efforts, and goals are consistently aligned with it.

I'm going to bring you back to chapter 2 for a moment when I shared the vision, mission, values, and goals that would drive Merchants' strategic direction.

- Our *vision* was to Enable the Movement of People, Goods, and Services Freely ("responsibly" would be added later).
- Our *mission* was to Provide the Most Comprehensive, Flexible, and Innovative Fleet Experience on the Planet.
- Our *values* encompassed Service, Integrity, Flexibility, Community, and Innovation.
- And our *goals* aligned with our six strategic imperatives that drove all our daily decisions along with our vision, mission, and values.

Critical to the complete alignment of our strategic direction was to make all this simple, understandable, and repeatable. To that end, our strategic direction was represented by a single word that was relevant to our industry:

F	**Fastest**-growing fleet company in North America
U	**Unique** business model with differentiated value to our clients
E	**Electric** vehicle evangelist with progressive ESG approach
L	**Leadership** positioned to fuel a $2.5 billion company
4	**4th** in the industry

Leadership Foundation

If a business were an F1 race car, the leadership foundation would be the steering wheel pointing the race car in the proper direction to move its strategic vision forward. In other words, it is leadership who translates the strategic direction into actionable initiatives, so that your people can bring it to life. Doing so requires, you guessed it, the right leaders, the right culture, and the right people.

High-Performance Culture

Organizations must hire and attract people who fit their culture. As we discussed in chapter 4, fueling your culture is vital to any transformation. And in this chapter, we are stressing the importance of building it into a high-performance system that is scalable and repeatable. At Merchants, we had cultivated a high-performance and innovative culture for our disruptive transformation, and our commitment to that culture required our continued focus on the right talent development and talent acquisition. Remember, not everyone within the company is going to align with a high-performance culture and some will opt out— accept this when it happens. There will also be people from outside the company who are attracted to a high-performance culture and will now seek to join your team: you have become a talent magnet.

Talent Acquisition and Development

Throughout the transformation process, your system is evolving and transforming, and adjustments and investments will be needed along the way. You will need to invest in your recruiting team, your career programs, your leadership training, ensure your benefits are competitive, and be able to highlight your culture so you can attract the high performers in and out of your industry.

It's critical that you actively listen for what your system is telling you. Do you need a marketing person with social media know-how because social media and branding are going to become a bigger part of your marketing strategy? If so, do you have someone within the company who is a strong marketer but lacks social media skills, and, equally important, can you support that team member in developing those skills? Are you moving in a direction that requires skills that no one in the company has and you also don't have the ability or time to develop those skills? If so, you will need to go into the market and hire that skill set.

At Merchants, we had some highly specialized finance roles for certain funding structures that no one in the company had ever worked on. In these instances, we needed to go into the market and quickly hire those skill sets. In either one of these two case examples, your talent must evolve with your system so that you are continually developing and attracting the talent who has the attributes, skills, and the ready, willing, and able mindset your culture demands. It's not easy, but if you build the right foundation, you will attract the right people.

Growth Engine

I like to think of a growth engine in business like the high-octane fuel that makes a company go from driving to and from the grocery store to speeding around an F1 racetrack (with occasional taps to the brakes when needed). In business terms, it is the driving force behind a business's ability to increase its revenue, customer base, market share, and overall market presence for accelerated and sustainable growth.

Let's review a few of the key ingredients to the high-octane fuel driving your growth engine:

- *Brand Equity:* Differentiated branding, marketing, and advertising strategies that contribute to increased visibility, brand awareness, and customer engagement, ultimately positioning you in the marketplace as a disruptor.

- *Sales Strategies:* Developing unique penetration strategies to acquire new customers with micro offerings to lower the barrier to entry and create new ways to do business with you.

- *Customer Focus and Retention:* Fundamental to any growth engine is maintaining focus on your existing customers while offering them new value and providing pilot opportunities to align more closely.

- *New Engines:* Introducing new and innovative products or services that stimulate growth by attracting new customers, retaining existing ones, and potentially opening new market segments.

- *Market Expansion:* Entering new geographic markets, reaching new customer demographics, or expanding the range of products/services offered to existing customers will increase growth.

- *Scaling Operations:* Efficiently scaling operations, whether through increased production capacity, optimized supply chains, or streamlined processes can contribute to business growth.

- *Technology and Digital Transformation:* Leveraging technology and digital tools to improve efficiency, enhance customer experiences, and tap into online markets can be a powerful growth engine.

- *Innovation with Employees:* Having a skilled, motivated, and innovative workforce can be a growth engine, as employees drive innovation, customer satisfaction, and overall organizational excellence.

- *Customer Feedback and Adaptation:* Actively listening to customer feedback and adapting products, services, or business models based on that feedback can lead to sustained growth by meeting evolving customer needs.

The right combination of these growth engines will vary based on a company's industry, market conditions, and overall strategic objectives. While at Merchants we continued to engage on some level with all the above components, I want to focus on Brand Equity, Sales Engine, and New Engines.

Brand Equity

Brand equity is all about how people see and feel about a brand—how much they trust it, what vibes they get, and if and why they'd choose it over other options. It's not just about being recognized; it's about having that unique energy that makes people willing to pay a bit more or keep coming back because they just love what the brand brings to the table. Your brand equity is your reputation, why people are drawn to you, and the good feelings it brings to your customers.

There are multiple components that come into play to create a strong and valuable brand presence in the minds of consumers. Here are a few key ones:

- *Brand Awareness:* This is the foundation. It's about how recognizable and familiar your brand is among your target audience. The more people know and remember your brand, the stronger its equity.
- *Brand Loyalty:* When customers keep coming back for more, you've hit the loyalty jackpot. Brand loyalty is a crucial component, reflecting the strength of the connection between your brand and its customers.

- *Brand Image:* This is the overall impression your brand leaves. It's a sum of all interactions and experiences people have with your brand, including advertising, customer service, and product usage.
- *Brand Trust:* Trust is the glue that holds it all together. If customers trust your brand, they are more likely to stick around. Trust is built through consistent delivery on promises and positive customer experiences.
- *Brand Differentiation:* What sets you apart from the crowd? Brand differentiation is about being distinct and unique in a way that matters to your target audience. It's your competitive edge.
- *Market Positioning:* Where you stand in the market matters. Your brand's position relative to competitors influences how customers perceive its value and relevance.
- *Marketing and Communication:* How you talk about your brand matters. Effective marketing and communication strategies contribute to building a positive brand image and shaping perceptions.

At the end of the day, your brand must fit your target market, so you attract the right customers. Our branding worked well for summer camp rentals, but that same branding would not attract the big players in the last mile market or instill the trust that we could provide them the fleet service they needed, when they needed it, and in the way they needed it.

For Merchants, our brand adjustments were extreme. For many years, we had a very small in-house marketing team and outsourced much of our marketing from strategy to web design and all development. As our vision grew and our company began to pursue more sophisticated markets, our logo, website, marketing materials, and sales training needed to match that level of sophistication. We needed to develop buyer journeys for different personas which required the introduction of new navigational paths to Merchants.

I can still remember when we were laying out our new customer journeys to go from marketing to summer camps to marketing the big three last mile companies and drawing pictures on whiteboards of what the customers looked like. Some of the long-term Merchants leaders laughed at what a "different world it was," and they were right. But they were also some of the biggest contributors to the transformation, because based on their tenured experience, they really knew how to juice the octane in the fuel. For instance, they knew our website was directed at small business owners, and now, we were pursuing the Fortune 100 and virtually everything needed to change.

We moved from seven websites to one, from marketing to small fleets to large fleets, from minimal sales training to a three-day sales summit full of marketing know-how and sales development. But the backbone of all of this was our vision—*enable the movement of people, goods, and services freely*—and values—*service, flexibility, and innovation*—and that was the glue we built our marketing around.

As a company builds success in a new market, continuous recalibration is needed in a variety of areas, and the same was true for Merchants. One area of marketing focus for us was speaking engagements. Before we began our transformation journey, our executives spoke at tradeshows within the industry, which was the right fit at the time. But with our decision to drive faster than our competitors, move into new markets, and differentiate ourselves from the pack, we needed to find new and bigger platforms to build our brand equity. To do this, we sought out speaking engagements at TechCrunch, *Bloomberg*, *Wall Street Journal*, and *Reuters*. Initially, Merchants was often the only speaker from our industry, providing us a captive audience. We saw engagement in these spaces as an opportunity that marketeers like to call "green fields and white space."

You've targeted your market and branded yourself accordingly; now it's time to build the sales engine that will capture it.

Sales Engine

Building a sales engine to capture your target audience is like gearing up for winning an F1 race. You need to have the right drivers behind the wheel, the right crew for the pitstop, and enough courage to hit the gas at opportunity and close the deal. At Merchants, we chose to move upstream and pursue larger clients, and to do this, we needed to tune (not rebuild) our engine.

- *Training:* we trained our sales teams in our vision, values, and new marketing strategies.
- *Teams:* we built our teams to be client focused.
- *Incentives:* we aligned all of our incentives for the overall teams to be successful.
- *Performance:* we instilled our high-performance culture and poured jet fuel on it for sales.
- *Support:* we surrounded our sales teams with all the support they could ever want (in some cases maybe more than they wanted).
- *Tools:* we provided our sales teams with tools needed to sell effectively.
- *Measurements:* we measured our success and failures through both leading and lagging indicators and pivoted as needed.
- *Innovation:* we constantly pushed the envelope to do better and come up with innovative ideas.
- *Yes:* we found ways to say "yes."

Our marketing team built the race car, sales teams drove the car, and our leadership team was endlessly on the lookout for new ways to make our engine run faster.

New Economic Engines

Creating new engines is all about developing innovative services and products that make your brand stand out and draw your customers in. It's the cool part of the business and your brand.

Here are key components to developing the system that not only supports your new engine but propels it around the track faster than any of your competitors.

- *Know Your Market:* Successful product or service innovation requires a deep understanding of the market from your perspective, your competitors' perspective, and your customers' perspective. Be open to and understand how to identify market signals, gaps, emerging trends, and unarticulated demands of your customers.
- *Stimulate New Thinking:* As we discussed in chapter 3 on leadership, successful companies bring in leaders and team members from diverse backgrounds to not only know your market as discussed before but to offer new perspectives that lead to new offerings through stimulated thinking.
- *Cultivate Cross-Functional Collaboration:* Innovation can't happen without collaboration. An aligned and interconnected approach will translate innovative ideas into marketable products and services.
- *Embrace Flexibility:* Building new engines in business requires rapid adjustments based on feedback, market dynamics, technological advancements, a willingness to say "yes," and flexibility.

- *Launch with Impact:* Effective communication—simple, understandable, and repeatable—of the new engine's features, benefits, and value proposition is a must for market acceptance. Vital to a launch's success is the ability to train your teams.

Developing new engines requires a real commitment to flexibility and innovation. At Merchants, we committed in a big way.

In chapter 4, I shared with you how Merchants intentionally worked to overcome the fixedness mindset that was holding the company back. Without taking that step, I knew we could not sustain the innovative culture necessary for launching new engines. We then created our own innovation department with its own INNOV8 committee, innovation coaches, and leadership team.

Firing up three of the four cylinders of our Transformation Systems—strategic direction, leadership foundation, and growth engines—to develop new products and services and create innovative ways to bring those products and services to market is what opened the door to our successful and scalable launch of our last mile program, truck rental, commercial sales, and our march upstream to larger clients. To truly transform systemically, new engines must be woven into the fabric of the company.

But first, we needed an operational machine to implement Merchants' new engine.

Operational Machine

Imagine a business is like a highly tuned racing engine, and to rev up those new growth engines, you need a well-oiled pit crew serving as an operational machine. It's not just about ideas; it's about having the right people, processes, technology, and the scalability to turn those ideas into big wins.

- *People:* You need the right people with the right skills, experience, and attributes to build a highly scalable and repeatable engine. Your team is the heart of the machine. Leadership might have the big ideas, but it is the people who bring those ideas to life, and it is the system that makes the good people great. Remember Brock Purdy!

- *Processes:* Think of processes as the gears that keep things running seamlessly. Smooth and clear operations ensure consistency and alignment. As you go through your transformation, there will be times when you "grind your gears" and that is normal and expected. What is important is that you focus on re-designing your processes, so the gears don't grind to a halt but instead accelerate through the apex of your growth.

- *Technology:* Technology is the accelerant to your operational machine that increases its effectiveness and efficiency if you engage it as an enabler to people and processes.

- *Scalability:* You have a big vision for your company's future, but you can't get from here to there in a day, a week, or even a year. You need a plan to gradually scale to reach each new stage of your vision. Scalability takes time, it requires some grinding on the gears, maybe even some duct tape from time to time, but as you build your system over time, your future will come into focus.

It's challenging when all systems are green—the market is hot, your sales engine is cranking, your systems are kicking in, and you're ready to grow 30, 40, 50 percent—but it's also important to have the IQ and EQ to continually balance between the gas and the brake so

143

that you don't grow so quickly that you burn out your people or damage your brand because you grew too fast or took too many risks.

When Merchants' lights were all green and we were building our systems out, we developed a four-year operational scalability plan that detailed how we would go from 200 cargo vans in year one for last mile to 3,000 in year two, 5,000 in year three, and 10,000 in year four. In other words, systems and scalability is a multi-phased and multi-year endeavor, requiring you to sometimes slow down to go fast.

Building Your Scalability Plan

Working through your scalability plan is sort of like teaching a quarterback how to run the offense. You don't give them the full playbook on day one and say, "Hey, we're going to run through this tomorrow." You share your base offense and have the offensive team work on it for a couple of weeks until the kinks are worked out and everyone is in alignment with the base plays. As the season progresses, you install more offensive plays, increase the sophistication, and introduce new concepts (or "wrinkles" as play callers call them). And week by week, you bring along the entire team, which instills a level of confidence and competence.

During Merchants' scalability progression, we started with one department, vehicle registrations, and made that successful over the course of six months. Once we knew how to do that well, we moved on to vehicle acquisition, then vehicle maintenance, and eventually, customer service and experience. In all, this took four full years, but we truly built a repeatable system that played to our strengths and our competitors' weaknesses.

Just like Kyle Shanahan, the head coach of the San Francisco 49ers and architect of their offensive system. He gives Mr. Irrelevant Brock Purdy as many plays, as much sophistication, and as many wrinkles as he can handle while doing a great job. Coach Shanahan also adapts his system to match the strengths of his team, just like your company should, and maximizes the weaknesses of his opponent, just like you will to your competitors. And as Brock taught us, it's not always the third pick in the draft that wins, it's the right person in the right system, and that is such an incredible lesson to learn as a leader of any transformation.

Can Your System Scale?

Having the right system in place is essential for any business's success, but if exponential growth is the endgame, the right system for right now must be able to adapt and evolve into the right system for scalability. If it can't, when that explosive growth happens, the business will hit a wall and be unable to keep up with its customers' demands. Companies of all sizes and ages can "hit the wall," if they don't continually adapt and adjust their business's strategic direction and the systems that support it. Just a few words earlier, I brought you back to Brock Purdy and how he and Coach Shanahan built a successful system; now I want to walk you through two abbreviated stories of Peloton in 2022 and Cabbage Patch dolls in 1983 as a few examples of companies that struggled to scale.

PELOTON

In 2012, the founders of Peloton made it their mission to "bring immersive and challenging workouts into people's lives in a more accessible, affordable, and efficient way." And they had great success. Then, the pandemic hit, and people who could no longer go to their gyms clambered for what Peloton was offering. The company was not prepared to scale to pandemic demands and customers waited months for their product. Then, gyms opened again and the clambering for Peloton's products and services took a dive seemingly overnight, creating a loss of $1.2 billion in just three months.

CABBAGE PATCH DOLLS

This hitting-the-wall scenario goes way back to 1983 and is one of the most famous buying crazes. Coleco's marketing team hit it out of the park when they created demand for the company's adorable, must-have dolls, but its manufacturing and logistics system just couldn't keep up. The result: parents pushing, shoving, and fighting with each other to make sure there would be a Cabbage Patch doll under their Christmas tree that year.

Peloton and Cabbage Patch dolls prove that even the most wanted products won't be successful long term if the systems behind them are not robust and built to scale. The dolls are no longer, but I am holding out hope for Peloton and that their new leaders will build a successful and scalable manufacturing system, just like their successful and scalable exercise system.

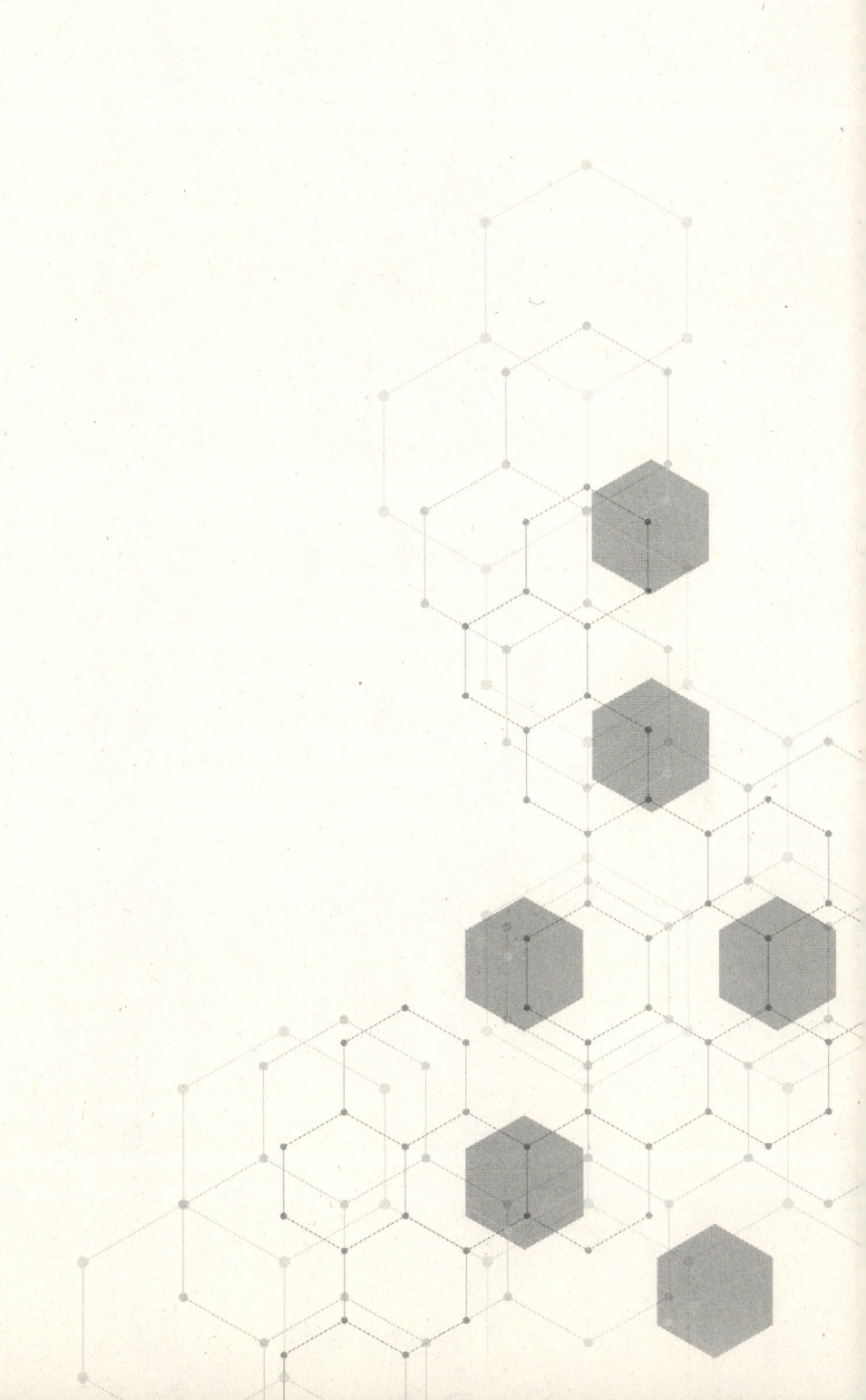

CHAPTER 7

PILLAR 5: IQ

A number of years ago, a CEO I was supporting and coaching was frustrated with one of her board members' inability to stop focusing on micro points and instead think strategically based on the big picture. It was at one of her company's first board meetings after a substantial acquisition, and they were discussing the strategy of transitioning two companies into one. The focus was on developing the right leadership team after the retirement of two of her top people. While this CEO understood that there are times that a focus on micro details is necessary, she also understood that this was not one of those times.

During the discussion, this board member repeatedly dragged her back to this one, incredibly small micro point. "Sarah, last quarter your inventory was down 1 percent while your sales were up 1.5 percent. Can you explain that? It seems like your inventory is off by 0.5 percent for the month."

Sarah assured me that she had been able to engage her EQ to calmly explain to the board member that (1) their number was correct, (2) she wasn't sure if it was a specific inventory miscalculation or something else but that they would review, and (3) right now, the focus needed to be on building the leadership team and implementing a successful transition or they would not garner the true value of acquiring the other company.

The board member still couldn't let it go. "Okay, but if you extrapolate this out, and this is a trend, and it continues to happen over the next eight quarters, inventory could be off as much as 4 percent."

This is an example of a person with a high IQ but who lacked the ability to see beyond the details and develop a big-picture strategy.

Now, if the intended focus had been a spreadsheet that itemized every single *potential* risk factor and a *potential* plan to address that *potential* risk factor, that board member was on the right track. But a company cannot succeed with that mindset. In fact, they'll be lucky to get out of the gate or down the field at all.

Imagine if every time a professional sports team lost a game, the owner said to the head coach, "We lost the game. Do you realize if we lose the next eight games, we'll have zero chance of making the playoffs? I can't risk it, you're out, I need different players, we need changes." Any long-term strategy they tried to implement would never take hold, and you can't make it to the playoffs without a long-term strategic plan to get you there, and in this CEO's case, they wouldn't be able to establish the right leadership foundation, Pillar 1, if the focus remained on the micro.

While not having enough IQ can become a challenge, it can also be problematic and impede growth when we become overly focused on processing and interpreting detailed information on a deep level. It's critical that leaders have the IQ to recognize and assess signals that inform the right path for the company's future, but they must also have the IQ to not overthink *potential* risks that are highly unlikely.

Becoming an EV Leader

Do you remember General Motors' Super Bowl commercial in 2021 starring Will Ferrell? He tells us that Norway leads the world in electric vehicles (EVs) and questions how America let that happen. He declares that America should be the global EV leader, and he's prepared to take action. He "drives" his EV to Norway (ends up in a shipping container headed for Sweden) and encourages his friends to drive their EVs to Norway, too—a "We'll show them" bravado.

Fast-forward to 2023, a year in which 1.4 million EVs were sold in the U.S. This number reflects an increase of 50 percent over 2022[9] (not sure how much of that can be attributed to the Will Ferrell effect). Even with that boost, the U.S. still only accounts for 7.6 percent of the EV global market, but significant strides are being made to increase those numbers.

In 2023, President Biden committed federal agencies to transition their light-duty fleets to all electric by 2027 and their medium- and heavy-duty fleets by 2035. Add to that the private big fleet players that are committing to EVs. Amazon has committed to having 100,000 electric delivery vehicles on the road by 2030. By that same year, 30 percent of Comcast's fleet will be EVs, and 100 percent of FedEx's parcel pickup and delivery vehicle purchases will be EVs.[10]

---

9   "Statement by U.S. Energy Secretary Jennifer M. Granholm on 2023 EV sales," January 5, 2024, https://www.energy.gov/articles/statement-us-energy-secretary-jennifer-m-granholm-2023-ev-sales.

10   Tom Swallow, "Top 10 companies driving commercial fleet electrification," August 9, 2022, https://evmagazine.com/top10/top-10-companies-driving-commercial-fleet-electrification.

With the push for more EVs, OEMs began ramping up their EV production. General Motors, as one example, announced plans to move to all electric vehicle sales by 2035.

At Merchants, we saw opportunity in these signals that suggested a significant future in EVs in the last mile segment of the fleet industry. When we assessed all the delivery vehicles that the major OEMs committed to building and all the companies and government agencies that said they were committing to EV fleets, it was clear that there was way more demand than supply. It was also clear that the explosion of EVs in the last mile market was on the horizon, and we decided Merchants would seize the opportunity to establish itself as an EV leader. But to be a leader, we needed to secure vehicles that didn't yet exist. It was time to fully tap into our transformation IQ to make that happen.

In the fleet industry, we must commit to x number of vehicles over x number of years before the vehicles are even built. We had to assess the availability of future EV allocations, which OEMs we could reserve these vehicles from, and the level of EV infrastructure that would increase over those same years. (Everyone can commit to utilizing millions of EVs by x date, but if the charging station infrastructure does not ramp up to meet those commitments, demand will fall off.)

Based on all that information and best estimated projections, we committed to ordering forty thousand EVs so that by 2025, 50 percent of our mobility fleet would be EVs, and by 2030, 50 percent of our entire fleet would be EVs.

Of course, committing to establishing an EV fleet in such a big way took much more than IQ. If we hadn't established our transformational leadership, if we hadn't cultivated the right culture and filled it with the right people, and if we hadn't provided those people with a transformational system that they could be successful in, we could have applied all the IQ in the world to the EV opportunity and failed to make it happen. But because we had healthy Pillars 1 through 4, Pillar 5, IQ, could be successfully employed to pave the way for Merchants to become an EV industry leader in the last mile market.

What Is IQ and Why Is It So Important?

We all know that our IQ is a number used to measure our apparent relative intelligence in comparison to others of the same age—it measures our ability to reason and problem solve. The higher the IQ, the higher one's ability to manipulate, process, and interpret information at a deeper level and a higher speed than others of the same age. What it doesn't measure is a person's practical intelligence, creativity, curiosity, and emotional readiness, all critical components of our overall intelligence.[11]

When I think of IQ, I break it down into four areas beyond the standardized test IQ score.

Industry IQ: A person who has studied and worked in a specific industry brings a certain level of intelligence about that industry. When I first entered the fleet industry, people, understandably, questioned my credentials to run a fleet company. I didn't have the industry IQ, but what I did have was the experiential IQ of turning around and transforming companies in a variety of industries. I didn't need a high fleet-industry IQ in that moment, because I knew I could draw upon the fleet-industry IQ of those around me. And the differing industry IQ I had as a fleet client helped to expand how Merchants viewed the fleet industry.

---

11   Jacque Wilson, "What your IQ score doesn't tell you," February 19, 2014, https://www.cnn.com/2014/02/19/health/iq-score-meaning/index.html.

Experiential IQ: Our experiences inform and expand our intellectual abilities and capacities. As we do, we learn and grow. Over my time with Merchants, through my experiences and study, I have developed my fleet-industry IQ. I have also intentionally brought in people with varying experiential and industry IQs to foster our culture of collaboration and innovation, beginning with the development of our leadership foundation.

Generational IQ: The generation we grow up in shapes our brains and the ways we connect with the world around us. As each new generation is confronted with new challenges, technologies, and ways of thinking and being, our ability to think logically and solve problems (our IQ) increases. This increase in IQ from generation to generation is known as the Flynn effect.[12] The takeaway for me here is the importance of drawing on the IQ of individuals from a wide range of ages. How a baby boomer intellectually approaches a challenge will be inherently different than a millennial's approach. Like industry and experiential IQ, I was intentional about the generational IQ of Merchants' leadership foundation. The members of our transformational leadership team ranged from twenty-nine to sixty-five years of age.

Academic IQ: Studies have linked a correlation between academic learning and increased IQ score.[13] As we study and absorb more knowledge, our general intelligence increases. I am a strong advocate for lifelong learning, and as I've shared, at Merchants, we are intentional about making academic learning available to every single member of our team on an ongoing basis.

---

12   Ibid.

13   Stuart J. Ritchie and Elliot M. Tucker-Drob, "How Much Does Education Improve Intelligence? A Meta-Analysis," Psychological Science 29, no. 8 (2018): 1358–1369, https://www.ncbi.nlm.nih.gov/pmc/articles/PMC6088505/#b ibr5-0956797618774253.

Once we decided to move into electrification, we realized we also wanted to be a more environmental, social, and governance (ESG)–focused company. This is when *responsibly* was added to our vision: Enable the Movement of People, Goods, and Services Freely and Responsibly. That required that we increase our knowledge of sustainability. Our head of training and development found a course on sustainability at Harvard, and as we began to dig into it, we said, "Time out. We need to put every leader at the director level and above through this course." We got some pushback, but we made it a requirement. If we were going to commit to becoming an ESG-focused company, we would all need to expand our academic IQ.

Everyone came back from the course with positive feedback. One of our salespeople reached out to me afterwards and told me that he had always viewed himself as a salesperson and had always tried to do a good job. "But," he said, "I feel like I now understand the higher purpose of putting EVs on the road and being a more progressive ESG company. I no longer look at it as selling a vehicle, because with EVs, what I am selling is sustainability and climate change and good governance." It was a truly cathartic time for the company. A time that almost overnight created a culture within leadership of sustainability. A culture that those leaders spread throughout Merchants. Sometimes when injecting IQ a bit of EQ sneaks in.

The collective IQ of a company is critical to its success and essential to a successful transformation. Remember when I talked about building Merchants' transformational leadership, and that team comprised a third of people from Merchants, a third from the fleet industry but outside of Merchants, and a third from outside of the fleet industry? Within those subsets, it's important to also include a mix of academic, experiential, and generational IQ levels. In doing so, you create a culture that finds solutions and knows how to get stuff done. And let's not forget the value of some good old-fashioned common sense.

One of my favorite successes of IQ is when Merchants concluded that to execute our strategic direction, we needed a complete rebrand of the company. Rebranding is no small task and must be done well or you risk tarnishing your brand or confusing your customers. But our strong, high-IQ, hardworking, millennial marketing leader led us through the brand change and brought us together as a team. Even the long-term Merchants team members who initially felt a bit "under attack" by the rebrand came to understand that how Merchants consistently and clearly presented itself to our clients, vendors, and stakeholders was critical to the success of our transformation.

Tuning into the Signals

Earlier in the chapter, I referenced the signals that indicated there was opportunity in the EV fleet market. In business, there are a multitude of "signals" that companies watch for and assess to determine how they will adapt and adjust to the dynamic changes in the world that will impact how they do or don't do business. Let's look at macro, adjacent, and core signals that businesses must watch, assess, and adapt for.

Macro signals: A macro signal is a dynamic timeline that shows important economic or financial trends, and it connects to how tradeable assets or investment positions perform. Macro signals are gathered from three main sources: economic data, financial market data, and expert opinions. Since there's tons of data out there, businesses utilize economic, finance, and statistical models to shrink the data into smaller, more meaningful indicators that provide a snapshot of what it all means.

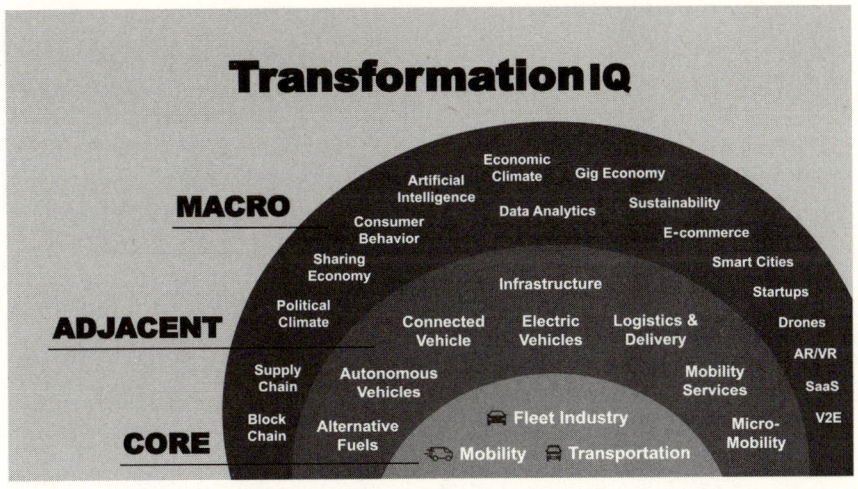

The macro signals between 2018 and 2023 are a great example of just how dynamic economic and financial trends can be in a relatively short period of time. In 2018, our macro signals of low inflation, interest, and unemployment rates indicated that our economy was doing well. Fast-forward twenty-four months to 2020, COVID hits, and a wholly different set of macro signals comes into play. Large swaths of people are suddenly essentially captive in their own homes forcing them to work, learn, and shop remotely. By the end of 2021 and through much of 2022, significant groups left the workforce (quiet quitting) or changed fields, leaving employers scrambling for employees to keep their businesses running.

By 2023, the impact of the economic and financial trends that occurred during the pandemic began to show up in different ways. Inflation rose, and to lessen its rise, the Fed increased interest rates. When inflation and interest rates rose, companies began laying off employees, and in this case, they also began to demand that employees return to the brick-and-mortar office if they wanted to keep their job. The emerging economic trends began to shift the employment power from employees back to employers.

These are all examples of macro signals. When you view macro signals, you must ask yourself, what do those signals mean for my business and what signals are happening in my industry? In other words, what are the adjacent signals to those macro signals?

Adjacent signals: An adjacent signal in business typically refers to relevant and related indicators, cues, or information that may be connected to a particular aspect or macro signal within the business environment. The additional insights that adjacent signals provide to the overall situation make them a critical component in decision-making processes and strategic planning.

For Merchants, some of the adjacent signals for the fleet industry during this tumultuous period included an increase in what was already a healthy market, last mile and home delivery. While everyone was captive in their homes, they bought virtually everything online from groceries to clothing and even cars. Meeting that unprecedented online demand required an accelerated increase in delivery vehicles and services. Combined, those increased pressures created a new macro signal: a breakdown in the supply chain. What were the adjacent signals to the fleet industry that we saw as a result? Fewer vehicles were being built and the ones that were being built had a significantly higher price tag. That meant that our access to purchasing vehicles when we needed them would be severely hindered. We needed to adapt to the change and procure vehicles before the window of opportunity closed.

A long-term result of that trend for auto makers was that they would not return to pre-pandemic levels of manufacturing, because they figured out that it was more cost effective to meet existing demand than to stockpile inventory that they historically had to quickly offload at discount prices at the end of each year. An adjacent signal for the everyday consumer is that they are no longer inundated with auto dealers' incentive ads in November and December to "save big" because "all inventory must go" with offers of "0 percent interest for seventy-two months" or "$7,500 off MSRP!" But when we look into the future, those ads will be back, and we will need to adjust again.

Recognizing and assessing these adjacent signals can help businesses make more informed decisions and develop a comprehensive understanding of the broader business landscape.

Core signals: Core signals generally refer to the fundamental indicators or key factors that are essential for understanding the overall health, performance, and direction of a business. These signals are critical for decision-making, strategic planning, and assessing the company's well-being.

Core signals may vary depending on the specific aspect of the business being considered, but they often include key performance indicators (KPIs) and metrics that directly impact the company's goals and objectives. Examples of core signals in a business include:

1. *Financial Metrics: Revenue, profit margins, cash flow, and return on investment.*
2. *Customer Metrics: Customer satisfaction, retention rates, and acquisition costs.*
3. *Operational Metrics: Efficiency measures, production output, and supply chain performance.*
4. *Market Metrics: Market share, competitive positioning, and industry trends.*
5. *Employee Metrics: Employee satisfaction, turnover rates, and productivity.*

Identifying and monitoring core signals is crucial for businesses to track their progress, identify areas for improvement, and make informed decisions that align with their strategic objectives.

Bringing It All Together

Let's look at some macro, adjacent, and core signals outside of the fleet industry and unrelated to the pandemic. Have you heard of "cable cutters"? Maybe you are one! Cable cutters are people fed up with the high cost of their monthly cable bill. That growing sentiment is the macro signal. The resulting adjacent signal is the increase in streaming service subscriptions. Cable cutters began subscribing to streaming services like Hulu and Netflix, and once they realized they could have five streaming services totaling $50 in monthly fees, they refused to keep paying $150 a month for cable and cut their cable services.

The core signal is the monthly economics: $150 for traditional bundled service vs. $50 or so for new unbundled services. On the flip side, the cable companies should be looking at less consumer demand, so be on the lookout for cable companies to be developing new streaming services or even acquiring streaming companies. But can you think of the biggest challenge for cable companies to react to cable cutters? Cable companies tend to stick with a stay-the-course strategy and that won't be enough to win the cable-cutting war.

A macro signal for a gas station could be fluctuating gas prices or a consistent decrease in gas prices. To compensate for the instability or the stagnant low prices, gas stations must look at and act upon the adjacent signals. For gas stations, that would be recognizing that when people pull into a gas station, they're hungry and thirsty. That signal is an opportunity to offer food and drink to their customers who initially came to fill their gas tank. Gas stations are a great example of macro and adjacent signals pushing not just a business but an industry to evolve and, in many cases, transform by leveraging the changing needs of their customers.

Back in 1964, advertising and marketing executive E. B. Weiss saw the future transformation of gas stations and was dismayed that the opportunity was not currently being seized upon. In his book *Management and the Marketing Revolution*, he laments, "There is growing recognition in the petroleum industry that the auto has revolutionized all retailing—except the retailing of the gas station! It is even seeping into the awareness of this industry that car traffic is now shopping traffic, and that more cars, driven by men as well as women, stop at gas stations every day than drive up to any other outlet, including perhaps the food outlet! No other retailer so completely wastes such a remarkable traffic count as does the gas station!"[14]

This was at a time when the first self-service stations were being introduced but wouldn't become the norm until the 1980s. And so began the evolution that led to the transformation from gas stations to convenience stores with gas pumps.

Today, I've stopped at "gas stations" and not even gotten gas. This generally occurs when I'm at a lacrosse tournament with my son. In the morning, I'll run over to the Cumberland Farms or Fuel Stop (or any of the many other convenience stores that also sell gas) next to the hotel and pick up cups of cereal, a little milk, a couple bottles of Gatorade and water, and maybe a Pop-Tart or two, for me. What I don't get is gas because I filled up my tank the day before. Some gas stations have brand-name fast-food chains in them like Subway and Dunkin', and some have their own little kitchens cooking up burgers and making salads for their customers. Who could have imagined that back in 1964?

I challenge you to take a moment to exercise your IQ and try to visualize what gas stations will look like in the future when we

---

14   "The history of self-fueling," February 28, 2024, https://www.convenience.org/Topics/Fuels/The-History-of-Self-Fueling.

finally do make the leap to all EVs—for starters, they will no longer be called "gas" stations. Charging an EV will take longer than gassing up a fuel-powered car—what adjacent signals will that extended time lapse create and how would you adapt your business to them? Let your mind wander and leverage all forms of IQ: gaming stations; on-site beauty services such as haircuts, nails, or massages; light shopping like a pop-up Lululemon; and maybe more full-service restaurants vs. fast food. What are your ideas?

Let's Go to Market

As you leverage your various forms of IQ—industry, experiential, generational, and academic—to set a new transformational path, I encourage you to think about it in phases. If you don't, it's easy to let the excitement and passion of the transformation become a runaway train. You must truly balance your IQ and EQ throughout the process or risk getting ahead of a methodical approach to your market. Remember, if you're going to eat an elephant, it's best to do it one bite at a time.

Once we determined, based on market research and assessment of Merchants' capabilities and gaps, that last mile would be one of our primary new growth engines that would fuel the next stage of our transformation, we had to determine how best for Merchants to enter the market, successfully sustain itself in that market, and eventually expand within that market.

We broke the process down into four phases:

Phase 1: Market Entry: A market entry strategy provides a roadmap of how a company will establish their presence in a new market. It considers who/what your target market is; what you intend to sell in that market; expected sales and profit margins for that market;

your company's goals—what your core capabilities and capability gaps are—to achieve those sales; and what the competitive landscape looks like—who are you up against, what do you have to offer that they don't? This is a tactical process that occurs over many months. It's important to remember that any decision to enter a new market must remain aligned with your company's strategic direction that is driven by your overall vision, mission, values, and goals.

When Merchants first entered the last mile market, we intentionally identified that the largest e-commerce company utilized thousands of small last mile companies to deliver their packages. Instead of approaching the large Fortune 100 company as a new start-up in the market, we chose to pursue one small last mile company that serviced the big e-commerce company to get us started. As I shared in chapter 6, we had begun to scale our systems based on our existing ability to:

- Acquire cargo vans
- Register cargo vans
- Transport vans to any zip code across the country
- Maintain vans while in use
- Transport vans back to base for resale or to new locations for rental to other clients
- Invoice and collect payments

We had developed this core capability nearly thirty years earlier for kids—we had a summer camp business that would deliver vans in June for summer camps and return them in September when the kids were back in school. Over that thirty-year period, we had grown our summer camp business from 100 passenger vans to nearly 1,500 passenger vans, a strong stay-the-course growth strategy. To make the transition from transporting people in passenger vans to transporting goods in cargo vans, we needed to start small, work out the kinks, and fine-tune our systems to meet the unique demands of the last mile market.

A few of these fine-tunings were simple. Where summer camps requested one or two vans per summer, small last mile companies required anywhere from five to fifty vans during peak season—think Santa Claus time! Other differences required greater adaptations. Summer camps transport their precious cargo with care and put limited miles on their vehicles which mean minimal wear, tear, or damages. But in the last mile space, where it's all about delivering as many packages as quickly as you can in both urban and rural areas, the cargo vans incurred greater wear, tear, and damages. As we learned this new market, we needed to continually engage our IQ to solve the challenges, both big and small.

Two years into the last mile market, we reached our pivotal Phase 1 metric: we had 3,000 active cargo vans in the last mile market that could seamlessly be delivered and picked up from any zip code across the country at any time of year. We were ready to expand within our new market. Before moving on, let's do a little comparison: thirty years to get summer camp rentals to 1,500 passenger vans and two years to grow last mile to 3,000 cargo vans. How is it possible that Merchants doubled the business in one-fifteenth the time? Just think of the market size of each of these markets and the timing of our new market entry.

Phase 2: Market Expansion: While market entry strategies provide a roadmap for businesses to establish their presence in new markets, market expansion strategies enable them to solidify their place in the market and achieve sustainable growth. Determining a company's readiness for expansion and measurement of success is done through a variety of data points derived from key performance indicators (KPIs), customer satisfaction surveys, and assessment of projected vs. actual revenue goals and profit margins.

In Phase 2, Merchants secured last mile business with bigger, well-established last mile providers. Over the next twenty-four months, we expanded our market share from 3,000 cargo vans to 10,000 cargo vans. When we reached our goal of 10,000, we were ready to move to diversify within the last mile market.

We were able to leverage this as a result of our rebranding efforts I shared a few pages back. Our new brand targeted last mile companies with solutions around peak season and variable fleets, a type of client our previous brand had not targeted. And remember the slightly reluctant long-term team members and leaders who weren't enthusiastic about our rebranding? Well, they got on board in years two and three when they saw the success of our dynamic marketing team.

Phase 3: Market Diversification: Once a company has entered a new market successfully and secured its foothold in the market through expansion, it's time to determine if there is an opportunity to diversify and the potential benefits and risks involved. Diversification has the potential to increase market share by leveraging core competencies, resources, and capabilities to attract new customers and to cross-sell or upsell to an existing customer base. Increasing market share in this way can shore up a company's ability to weather cyclical changes, economic downturns, and distinguish themselves from their competitors.

As a company assesses the potential benefits of diversification, it must also assess its risks. Can the company sustain the higher costs associated with the diversification from a marketing, sales, production, distribution, management, and logistics perspective? Will this diversification strengthen the company's alignment with its vision, mission, values, and/or goals or put it at risk of decreasing its alignment?

When we determined our readiness to diversify, we had 10,000 active cargo vans in the last mile market. How would we diversify? By expanding our customer's fleet options. To our last mile services, we added box trucks and then eventually, we moved into what is called the "middle mile" (delivery to fulfillment centers which would then load the goods onto cargo vans and box trucks for the "last mile" of delivery) with the addition of tractor trailers.

The metric we set to determine when we were ready to move to Phase 4 was 15,000 cargo vans, box trucks, and other specialty vehicles. When we reached that milestone twenty-four months later, we hit the

brakes and reassessed. You may have noticed that each phase was an increment of twenty-four months. That was not intentional simply because we didn't know if Phase 1 would be successful until we actually took the calculated risk and did it. But it is interesting to let your IQ wander on the symmetry of progressing through each phase within the same time span.

Phase 4: Market Globalization: Global marketing involves packaging and selling your products and services beyond the boundaries of the company's home country. Thanks to advancements in technology and the dawn of e-commerce, globalization is no longer only for heavy hitters like McDonald's and Coca-Cola. Today, companies of all types and sizes can seize the opportunity to globalize their products and services.

As with all strategies, market globalization offers a range of benefits that can positively impact businesses, economies, and societies. The most obvious is expanded market reach that enables companies to increase revenue by tapping into new consumer demographics and get those goods and services into the hands of people who might otherwise not have access. Because globalization necessitates the collaboration and exchange of ideas with people and companies around the world, it fosters innovation in a big way which increases a business's competitive edge. Globalization also increases a company's access to resources and capital, helping facilitate business expansion and development.

Just as companies must best determine the growth strategy that is right for them—stay the course, evolve, or transform—they must also determine what markets are right for them. Merchants' plan for Phase 4: globalization was to expand our market reach in North America by entering the markets in Canada and Mexico. But when we reached the ready-for-Phase-4 milestone, we had to say time out. The truth was we were barely keeping up with Phases 1, 2, and 3, and we determined that entering the global market at that point would not be beneficial to Merchants.

We had clients asking if we could service their needs in Canada, Mexico, and London, but we had the IQ to realize that while we could probably make it happen, we did not feel that we would be able to maintain full alignment with one of our core values: Service. Our brand promise is that we will provide high-quality service at every point in our customers' fleet journey with Merchants. We were honest with those customers. We thanked them for the opportunity but let them know that our commitment is to do a great job for them every time, and if we said "yes" now, we'd be able to do a good job, but in six to twelve months, we'd be ready to do a great job. I will tell you, there were times that it was challenging to muster the IQ to say "no" when all I wanted to say was "Yes, full steam ahead!"

In chapter 1, I first mentioned my daily decision of gas or brake. It continued to be my biggest daily decision throughout Merchants' transformation. I can tell you from experience that the gas or brake decision is never more critical than when all systems are go and you and your team are doing laps around the track successfully. Tapping the brakes when everyone is on a high requires a leader to really lean into their IQ to adjust the speed at just the right moment and for just the right amount of time. It also requires the leader to draw on their EQ to help everyone on the team understand why the brakes need to be applied and how it will help the company be more successful in the long run. Let me leave you with this: EQ is often the more challenging pillar to lean into.

CHAPTER 8

PILLAR 6: EQ

It was 1997 and as a leader of a 1,200-person sales team at a Fortune 100 company, the team was overachieving. Whatever business metric was dished out as a goal by senior leadership, my warrior sales force of 1,200 strong smashed it out of the park. As a leader, I was flying high, so naturally, I jumped at the chance to go through an executive coaching program complete with a 360-degree assessment. Up until this point, I had always been focused on achievements, and I looked forward to the glowing assessment I was sure I would receive.

It didn't pan out quite the way I anticipated. Here's how the one-on-one with my executive coach unfolded:

"Brendan, your leaders all scored you off the charts; leader after leader told me about how you do what is asked of you and more," said the executive coach. "Your team members love you too. They will run through brick walls for you. Your people truly feel appreciated and rewarded," the coach continued.

"Your peers on the other hand …" the coach continued.

And here's where the other shoe dropped …

"They don't care for you that much. Here are some ways they described you: non-cooperative, me-focused, unable to see the bigger picture, solely focused on his team, and someone that really needs to mature," said the coach. "What are your thoughts on this, Brendan?" the coach asked.

I sat speechless, dumbfounded, confused, and completely unaware that my peers, the people who really mattered to making the sales team successful in my current role, harbored such negative feelings toward me. I struggled to understand how they could feel this way when I was performing so well and working tirelessly to drive our growth and stock price. And I wondered how I could be so liked by one group and so disliked by another.

Rather than fill this chapter with my shortcomings, I'll keep it simple. I had all the IQ to do my job, but I lacked the emotional intelligence (EQ) to lead with depth and sustainability. My capacity for self-awareness did not extend beyond the borders of my team. My single-minded focus on goal achievement for me and my team severely hindered my capacity for empathy, and I definitely did not understand the need for, let alone how to balance between, gas and brake—I was all gas all the time.

This executive coach and coaching program completely changed not only who I would become as a leader, but the very trajectory of my career and more importantly my life. In that one moment in time, my peers and coach taught me more than all my combined performance reviews prior and since. I simply cannot thank my peers from 1997 enough for waking me up to the power of EQ. My sincere thanks to all of you!

Project Cool

I can't think of a time that required more EQ than when leading any company through the global COVID pandemic. When the pandemic hit, leaders didn't just need the EQ to help employees do their jobs better—and oftentimes, do it in entirely new and unexpected ways—it required us to understand how our employees were navigating this time of great challenge to their social, mental, physical, and financial health. And while successful leaders do take into consideration their employees' social, mental, physical, and financial well-being during non-crisis times, COVID pushed that understanding beyond consideration into a top priority.

It was easy for all of us to be consumed by the fear, uncertainty, and doubt that COVID had forced upon us, and any CEO's number one job as the company's leader was to decelerate the FUD and lower the emotional temperature. Leadership teams needed to convey a sense of calm, cool, and collected emotions in a way that could cascade throughout the company. To meet that need, Merchants launched Project Cool.

The "C" was for COVID and the word "Cool" served to reflect the sense of cool, calm, and collected emotions we were intent on creating. Project Cool didn't eliminate the stress that COVID was creating—we, like most companies, were having to adapt how we did business with every new obstacle the pandemic threw at us—but it significantly helped us address those stresses in a calm and organized way: a way that diffused the FUD.

As you may recall, COVID was not just a change for companies, it was a dramatic change for every aspect of living. Our employees had far bigger challenges than working remote or learning Zoom or any of the other changes to their work life. People were focused on their children learning from bedrooms and living rooms, being out of school and struggling socially, their elderly parents in nursing homes, their friends and family that were being laid off or put on furlough due to business challenges, and so much more. In my opinion, this was a time that required more emotional intelligence than any other point in my lifetime.

Project Cool's number one priority was transparency. We were all navigating this new territory together and the best way to assuage those natural fears of the unknown was to inform *everyone* of what was happening and the resulting impact. We've always been transparent, but pre-COVID, not everyone needed to know everything—now, we wanted to share as much as possible with every member of the team. Education was our second priority. We would be upfront about what was going on *and* educate everyone on how we would move forward and everyone's role in that forward momentum.

We knew that if we were going to commit to transparency and education, we also needed to figure out the best modes and frequency of communication to make sure that happened. Remember, this was during a time when most companies were primarily working remotely. Gone were the opportunities to just check in with someone at the office to see how they were doing or offer them words of encouragement in real time, and there were no impromptu in-person team huddles to brainstorm solutions.

Our Project Cool dashboard always reflected the realities of our challenges. "Guys, we have 256 clients who have been shut down. We don't know how long that shut down will last, but here's how we're going to help them through this period." All of this was communicated through our new, company-wide, weekly Zoom meetings.

You know what else was communicated in those meetings? Sentiments of "We got this," "How are you holding up?" and "How can I/we help you?" It wasn't just how do we keep moving Merchants forward, it was also how do we keep our individual team members moving forward in their personal and professional life. Deeper personal connections were made during this time, because we literally saw into people's lives. Everyone was talking from their kitchen, living room, their personal space. And we would meet their kids, spouses, and other family members who were now home with them.

These Friday-afternoon Zooms served as both work updates and pre-weekend social hours. From time to time, they would include talent shows, bring your kid to Zoom, pet show-and-tells, and the occasional game show. Comments from team members like, "Thanks everyone, I really needed that today" showed us we were on the right track. Each week we had to assess what the next week might bring and how we could best prepare for it. It was our EQ that we relied upon most for guidance during this period. And remember my younger self in 1997? That leader would have thought these were not productive and wouldn't lead to achieving our goals—in life and leadership, we all truly get a chance to grow, and to grow emotionally is one of the most rewarding types.

We knew our people were hurting and needed to feel connected and listened to and understood and lifted up, and it was our responsibility to make that happen as best we could. During the pandemic, companies either got pulled apart or pushed together. At Merchants, we chose to fully engage our EQ and push together, and it was that choice and the mindset and processes of Project Cool that really cemented our culture. It made us stronger as a team and as a company.

The Project Cool EQ mindset and process slowed our emotions and our heart rates, enabling us to tap into our IQ—the other critical component to weathering COVID—to find the unique solutions this unprecedented time called for.

What Is EQ and Why Is It So Important?

EQ, or emotional intelligence, refers to the ability to recognize, understand, manage, and effectively navigate one's own emotions and the emotions of others. Through his research, psychologist and author of *Emotional Intelligence*, Daniel Goleman, has identified the following five key personal and interpersonal skills involved in emotional intelligence:

1. *Self-Awareness:*
    - Recognizing and understanding one's own emotions.
    - Having a realistic self-assessment and understanding one's strengths and weaknesses.
    - Demonstrating a capacity for self-reflection.

2. *Self-Regulation:*
    - Maintaining composure in stressful situations.
    - Controlling impulsive reactions and thinking before acting.
    - Adapting to change with flexibility and resilience.

3. *Empathy:*
    - Demonstrating an understanding of others' emotions and perspectives.
    - Actively listening to others and showing genuine interest in their feelings.
    - Offering support and compassion to those in need.

4. *Social Skills:*
    - Building and maintaining positive relationships with others.
    - Effectively communicating and resolving conflicts with tact and diplomacy.

- Collaborating well within a team and fostering a positive group dynamic.

5. *Motivation:*
   - Being driven by intrinsic motivation and a passion for personal and professional growth.
   - Setting and achieving challenging goals with perseverance.
   - Maintaining a positive attitude even in the face of setbacks.

Goleman went on to research the connection between EQ and effective performance among leaders. When he calculated the ratio of technical skills, IQ, and EQ as components of what makes leaders outperform, he discovered that EQ was twice as important as technical skills and IQ, no matter the job level; and the higher up the ladder a leader rose as a star performer, the higher their level of EQ. When comparing A-list leaders with the average ones in top positions, almost 90 percent of the differences in how they performed were because of EQ rather than IQ.[15]

Let's look at examples of some high-EQ leaders.

Marc Benioff, the co-founder and CEO of Salesforce, is renowned for his commitment to corporate social responsibility and fostering an inclusive culture. He actively promotes employee well-being and has gained recognition for his philanthropic initiatives. This approach has consistently positioned Salesforce as a leading workplace globally for over a decade, contributing to one of the most extraordinary success stories in contemporary business.

---

15 Daniel Goleman, https://www.danielgoleman.info/; Daniel Goleman, "What makes a leader?" 2004, https://hbr.org/2004/01/what-makes-a-leader.

Benioff's emphasis on leading with a healthy dose of EQ has translated into impressive business outcomes. The company has experienced significant workforce expansion, boasting over seventy-eight thousand employees, along with notable growth in net income and shareholder returns. From 2017 to 2022, Salesforce's net income demonstrated a remarkable compound annual growth rate of 35 percent, and its five-year total shareholder return reached 57 percent.[16]

Jeff Weiner, the former CEO of LinkedIn, is known for promoting empathetic leadership and prioritizing employee well-being. He frequently underscores the importance of compassionate management and leading with emotional intelligence. In 2019, Glassdoor recognized Jeff as one of the top CEOs, achieving an impressive 97 percent approval rating. This marked his fifth consecutive year leading Glassdoor's rankings.[17]

When discussing the key to success, Jeff consistently points to the importance of compassion and what it means to lead with it.

It meant walking a mile in the other person's shoes and understanding their hopes, their fears, their strengths, and their weaknesses. And it meant doing everything within my power to set them up to be successful.

Jeff is another example of EQ-driven leadership that has translated into successful business outcomes. Taking over as CEO in mid-2009,

---

16   Dan Bigman and Ted Bililies, "Benioff's way: a conversation with salesforce founder and 2022 CEO of the year Marc Benioff," https://chiefexecutive.net/benioffs-way-a-conversation-with-salesforce-founder-and-2022-ceo-of-the-year-marc-benioff/.

17   Larry Kim, "Get to know LinkedIn CEO Jeff Weiner: 10 facts you haven't heard," September 23, 2019, https://www.inc.com/larry-kim/get-to-know-linkedin-ceo-jeff-weiner-10-facts-you-havent-heard.html; Lisette Voytko-Best, "LinkedIn CEO Jeff Weiner ending 11-year run," February 5, 2020, https://www.forbes.com/sites/lisettevoytko/2020/02/05/linkedin-ceo-jeff-weiner-ending-11-year-run/?sh=7a8561401a83.

the company went public in 2011 with a $4 billion valuation and was later acquired by Microsoft in 2016 for $27 billion.

The great news is, although we are all born with varying levels of EQ, we can develop and increase our EQ over time. Self-awareness, recognizing your own emotions in response to people and scenarios, is the first step. If you don't know what's truly triggering your heightened emotions, you won't be equipped to regulate those emotions. Developing your EQ is a lifelong process. I have been working on mine for a couple of decades, and I still need to check in with myself when approaching certain scenarios, as I highlighted at the beginning of this chapter.

Embracing Your EQ to Leverage Your IQ

Remember those 256 clients we let our employees know were shutting down indefinitely during COVID? That was just one example of the impact the pandemic had on Merchants. We are in the fleet transportation business, and when limo companies suddenly ground to a halt in the spring of 2020, their need for fleet services did too. Like our employees, our clients were also hurting. They were trying to adapt and adjust, often on the fly, while simultaneously trying to figure out how to stabilize their business for the long term. We needed to draw on our EQ to listen to our clients, to understand their needs, and to help them as best we could.

When our clients' services were grounded, our leadership team got in a room and brainstormed (as we did every afternoon from three o'clock to five o'clock during the height of COVID) how we could solve that day's challenge. We didn't know how long the services these companies provided would be stalled, but we knew it would likely be at least through the end of 2020. We began with, "At the end of the day, our clients are leasing *x* number of vehicles from Merchants, they have no revenue coming in for the foreseeable future, and if they are still able to pay us now, they won't be able to do it for much longer. So, what's the best thing we could do for these clients?"

I still remember somebody in the room said, "We take all the vehicles back and get them out of the leases."

Our CFO's instinct was to say, "We can't do that, we're going to lose money."

The team's collective response was, "We can do it, and we should do it."

Now that we had successfully traversed the EQ chasm, it was time to intentionally employ our IQ to figure how to make it happen.

People were still buying pre-owned cars at this point, so we arranged a deal for each of our clients that needed to get out of their leases and turn in their cars to do so at a slight discount. With the discount, we would take their vehicles to the auction and sell the vehicle and the discount would cover the auction fees and our team's internal costs. The client no longer had vehicles they weren't using and more importantly couldn't pay for. By making these pre-owned vehicles available at auction, Merchants also helped buyers who could not procure the new vehicles they needed when supply chain issues came into play. By employing both our EQ and IQ, Merchants helped our clients solve the future problem their unpaid debt would have created and guaranteed a strong relationship long after COVID was gone, and the good times were rolling again.

I made some of those client calls to let them know how we were looking to help them, and I remember how relieved and appreciative they were. Now, with our client's emotions dialed down and their FUD tempered a bit, they were better equipped to tap into their IQ to strategize how they could best move forward. Because we took care of our clients, because we had their back in their time of need, once businesses opened back up, it was Merchants they returned to for their fleet services. The trust we had built with them garnered a level of loyalty that money simply cannot buy. The trust we continued to earn throughout the pandemic and post-pandemic remained strong, because our vision and values never wavered.

In the end, we chose to take a significant negative: our clients would be unable to pay us for x number of months, and we turned it into something much more manageable for our clients: we alleviated the pressure of their lease commitments, and we created a way for Merchants to recoup some of the loss of those canceled leases: we sold the vehicles we took back at breakeven or a small profit. Making that happen required significant EQ and IQ. I think by now you know what else I am going to say it required:

- Pillar 1: Leadership
- Pillar 2: Culture
- Pillar 3: People
- Pillar 4: Systems

Without the right leadership, culture, people, and systems in place, the ability and opportunity to employ our EQ and IQ so successfully as a team and in such a dynamic and uncertain environment would simply not have been possible.

While the fleet industry fell 17 percent during the pandemic, Merchants grew 38 percent for a 55 percent differential, which I attribute to EQ and the ability to stay cool and focused on what we needed to do and the IQ to figure out how we needed to do it.

Gas or Brake

"Brendan, you're all about growth, disruption, and innovation, but right now, it seems like you're working from a fixedness mindset."

Yup, those words were said to me by one of my team members. My EQ understood their perspective. We were doing well with our first last mile client, and we were all thrilled with our early success. Couple that with the fact that we had intentionally cultivated a culture of innovation and fearlessness, and now, I was telling everyone we needed to slow down. In my less experienced days, that would have frustrated the heck out of me, too. But my experiential IQ developed over my years as a transformational leader is what informed

my decision to tap the brakes in this moment. Now, I needed to translate that understanding to my team.

In chapter 7, I outlined our four-phase go-to-market strategy for our new last mile growth engine, and it was the talking through that strategy that enabled team members to understand the need to tap the brakes in this moment. Many of our team members

wanted to grow faster, take on new clients, and enter the next phase. Trust me, I wanted to as well, but my experiential IQ was instinctually telling me to tap the brakes.

We were crossing over from Phase 1 to Phase 2 as we approached 3,000 cargo vans on the road. We had dozens of prospect opportunities available to us at the time, but we made the decision to stick to our phased strategy that kept us relevant to a smaller number of clients. And that is how we reached our next milestones of 5,000 and 10,000.

A significant factor contributing to this decision was the supply chain shortage of vehicles because of COVID. Cargo vans especially were in short supply requiring us to match the limited number of vans and our best possible prospects and clients with precision.

When leadership gathered at the end of each day for our Project Cool meetings at 3:00 p.m., I would often reiterate our phased approach and give people a chance to listen, advocate, probe, agree, and disagree until we all aligned on the path forward. It was a vital exercise that provided team members a forum to openly voice their concerns, ideas, and frustrations.

When a company goes through a transformation, one of the top challenges a leader must contend with is sequencing. Although you know the eight things you must do to transform and you are eager to act on them all immediately, if you do all eight things at a pace that your people and systems can't keep up with, your transformation will fail. Innovation and change have emotional components to them. The sequencing balance requires a leader to channel their EQ to be aware of what's driving their own emotions and what's driving the emotions of their team members—remember two components of EQ from Goleman: self-awareness and self-regulation.

For some, that emotion may be driven by discomfort and sometimes outright fear of letting go of the familiar, uncertainty of what comes next, and doubt as to whether they can adapt. For others, their emotion might be driven by their excitement of making the vision a reality as quickly as possible. Leaders must be tuned into their employees' EQ. If not, the

person motivated by fear of letting go may slow down progress while the person highly motivated by reaching the endgame may push too fast. If one individual or team is applying the brakes to the company's overall goal and vison while another individual or team is hitting the gas for maximum speed, people and systems will break down and transformation will not occur.

It is the leader who must decide the gas and brake for the company.

When a leader understands what is driving motivation and behaviors, they can work to raise the overall EQ of the company and bring everyone's emotions and motivations into alignment with the company's overall vision.

A good example of sequencing and pacing your change management process is when I first arrived as CEO of the company after stepping off the board. If you remember, Merchants was a confederation of companies, and I had a vision of collapsing all the companies into one. But I didn't do this all at once. The process took a full twelve months to complete. Why? Because if I had attempted to push it through right away, the company would not have been able to keep up with the pace of change. And when people can't keep up, they lose the feeling that they are "part of the change" and instead feel like the change is "being done to them."

Transformations, disruptions, and innovations require a phased and sequenced approach. In other words, bring them on the journey!

A key to moving forward as one company was centralizing our duplicative operations. You might think this is crazy, but our strategy to centralize operations took place over four years. It would have been great if we could have done it in six months or a year, but again, if you give more gas than your people and systems can handle, you won't be successful because (1) you will demotivate your people and eventually burn them out and (2) you will fail to see what's falling through the cracks, before it becomes a crater too big to fill.

When your sequencing works in tandem with the capabilities of your people and systems, you will see the tiny cracks that occur along the way and be able to fill and stabilize them in real time. If you don't, six or twelve months in, you may be scratching your head wondering why you've lost key team members and/or clients.

The Roadmap to Centralization

So, here's how we centralized operations. First, we needed to build the necessary architecture for this new organization and a new go-to-market strategy. The building of this architecture would begin with our leadership foundation (Pillar 1). Once that was solid, we focused our efforts on communicating Merchants' new vision and organizational changes to every member of our team to drive our transformational culture (Pillar 2). Next, we invested in our people (Pillar 3), converting the neutral majority we talked about in chapter 5 to raving fans while providing opportunities and incentives to upskill to the level Merchants' transformation required.

Once that structure was in place, we were ready to begin to centralize our first fleet business function: registration. While building the structure took months to complete, the next phases of our centralization would roll out over the next few years. Registration was the function we determined would be the easiest to centralize, and so, that is where we began. We did have some resistance which I shared with you in chapter 4, but overall, the process went smoothly. That success gave us the green light to hit the gas and roll out the next phase of the organization's centralization.

The next function in the centralization lineup was fleet maintenance. This one was a bit tougher because each of the seven companies under Merchants had their own maintenance departments and their own way of doing things. Even though vehicle maintenance is vehicle maintenance, because they operated independently of each other, they also had separate and distinct cultures, and melding cultures comes with its own unique emotional challenges. By leveraging our EQ, we held design sessions with the different maintenance groups to truly give them

a voice in the process and to understand the differences. Oftentimes, we found that the best solution was an integrating component of each of the groups. The final outcome was a new fleet maintenance team and process.

As each function was successfully centralized, we hit the gas on the centralization of the next function in the lineup which included transportation, field marketing, account management, and sales. The last function to be centralized was our most client-facing function: sales. That sequencing was intentional. We wanted to learn to function as one company internally—to work all the kinks out—before we fully transitioned our most client-facing function. Guess how deep into the transformation we were before we made this transition? We were in our fifth year. Yes, year not month. My point here is simple: work things out internally and behind closed doors before you bring it out into the market. This may seem intuitive when you read it here but trust me there is a strong desire to move on the external client side early. Always remember to leverage your growing EQ and IQ.

A few key takeaways about EQ before we move forward:

1. Balance EQ and IQ for your best transformational changes.
2. EQ starts by listening and learning to make the best decisions.

3. Situational awareness will lead you to high-EQ moments.

4. Transformations require you to move faster than your competitors but not faster than the change your team can keep up with.

5. When in doubt, ask.

EQ and a Side of Sneakers

I'd like to wrap up the power of EQ with two words: Air Jordan. Whether you're a basketball player, a basketball fan, or someone who knows nothing about basketball, you know what an Air Jordan sneaker is. And if you are a recreational basketball player or avid fan, just the idea of putting on Air Jordans makes you believe, even if just a smidge, that you could leap, pass, and shoot like Michael Jordan. The Air Jordan evokes emotions that transport it far beyond a sneaker and into something truly magical. Why? Because in 1984, when Nike was pigeon-holed as a "running shoe" company, and they were trying to make a name for themselves in the basketball shoe segment, they supercharged their EQ and created a sneaker, partnership, and marketing strategy that would not only catapult Nike's success beyond their wildest dreams but serve to disrupt the face of sports marketing and athlete endorsement deals forever.

At the time, Converse and Adidas were at the forefront of the basketball shoe industry. They were signing the big names like Larry Bird and Magic Johnson—known fan favorites. When Nike first set their sights on Jordan, he was still playing college ball and he was a big Adidas and Converse fan. In fact, Jordan admits that he never wore a Nike shoe until he signed with Nike.[18]

---

18   Josh Peter, "Error Jordan: key figures still argue over who was responsible for Nike deal," September 30, 2015, https://www.usatoday.com/story/sports/nba/2015/09/30/error-jordan-key-figures-still-argue-over-who-responsible-nike-deal/72884830/.

It was an uphill battle for Nike to be sure, and who led the charge and had the biggest impact on how it all played out depends on who you ask. But at the end of the day, while their IQ may have been screaming not to hedge all their bets on a *potential* star, in a segment of the industry in which they had not had success with a shoe that had not yet been created, their EQ outweighed the risk and enabled them to take the leap that would make history.

Nike's first EQ test was getting Jordan to sign with a non-basketball powerhouse whose sneakers he had no interest in wearing. Talk about a steep hill to climb. But they could see the potential of this rising star and they knew they needed to offer something vastly different than what their competitors were offering to the big-name players. Instead of convincing Jordan to "sell" Nike by wearing their sneakers in the same way that Bird and Johnson were "selling" Converse by wearing Converse shoes, Nike flipped that standard concept. Nike would "sell" Jordan; they would sell the dream of leaping into the air like Jordan with a shoe designed just for him. That concept and Jordan's financial position in this partnership (it was no longer just an endorsement contract but a full-blown partnership that would last more than thirty years) would seal the deal. The other stroke of genius by the Nike executive team? They leveraged their EQ to recognize that Mrs. Jordan, Michael's mother, played a significant role in the decision-making process.

Nike then leveraged the emotional pull to "be like Mike" by wearing Air Jordans—"It's gotta be the shoes"—to stratospheric success, and the rest they say is history.

Transforming a company is not all about the price or having the best product; sometimes it's about recognizing who your employees and consumers are, pushing away the logic IQ is sending your way, and meeting their emotional desires and needs. Building EQ in your company to do what's best for your customers will ultimately be in the company's best interest too.

Now, we're ready to move on to Pillar 7: Flexibility.

CHAPTER 9

PILLAR 7: FLEXIBILITY

It was 9:00 a.m. in Paris, and I was sitting in a windowless conference room dressed in my best suit ready to meet with the French Employees Union to negotiate our annual contract with them. Without any fanfare, the union reps walked into the room and took their seats. The union director sat directly across from me and began to list the union's large number of requests—a list they had sent to me in advance that included more PTO, a shorter work week, upgraded cars, higher salaries, and bigger bonuses. I listened patiently, first to the director in French and then to the English translator, and then I channeled my IQ, EQ, and flexibility and offered what I believed was a reasonable response.

"I've had a chance to review everything that you're asking for and I've also had the opportunity to assess the requests against our cost model. If we agree to all your requests, continuing to work within France would require us to do so at a significant financial loss. Clearly, that model would not be sustainable for our company. Nor would it sustain the jobs of the employees you represent. So, let's figure out what we can do and what we can't do that both keeps the union happy and enables us to develop a sustainable long-term business in France. We can give you upgraded cars and increased salaries, but if we provide those, we can't also offer a shorter work week, because then we won't have enough billable service hours for our clients."

The union director's response was, "It's not my job to make money for your company. My job is to represent the union workers which means securing the best cars, the best salaries, and the least number of hours worked possible."

"I understand," I said, "but here's the thing: if you tell me our only option is to give you everything your union demands, we will no longer be able to do business in France and all the union workers employed by us will lose their jobs. We simply cannot continue to operate in France if it means we must operate at a significant loss. Continuing in France will require some compromise and flexibility on both our parts."

I attempted to dialogue about options, but every attempt was met with the same response from the director, "Making money for your company isn't our focus. Our focus is on the best conditions for our workers." After several rounds of talks, I said, "I just want to make sure I understand that you're saying that if we don't meet all your demands starting on this date, your workers will not show up for work. Do I have that correct?"

His answer was an unequivocal, "Yes."

"Well, then," I said, "when our annual service contract comes up with a manufacturing supplier, we will put in all your requests and dramatically increase our price to them, but I know they will terminate our contract and move our business to a different supplier." And the union rep simply stated, "Then you will be out of business like you deserve." A few short weeks later, we were in our annual manufacturing auction portal, bidding on the service work. We entered the new contract prices, and sure enough, the business moved to our biggest competitor. And that was that.

Because the union was completely inflexible, at the end of the contract, we were forced to close up shop in France and nearly one hundred employees lost their jobs. Now, as the CEO of a global company, France was not the only country we contracted with that was unionized. In fact, that same year I had a similar challenge in Germany with our German Works Council. But with a different outcome for one reason: FLEXIBILITY.

To begin with, the conference room in Germany was far more inviting with warm welcomes from the German council members and a nice array of breakfast offerings. While there was an interpreter present that we occasionally relied on for clarification, the meeting was conducted in English. Much like the French Union, the German Works Council had provided me, in advance, a list of requests which the council director reviewed at the opening of the meeting.

My initial response was much the same as the one I had provided to the director in France, letting them know that I wanted to do what I could for them but that I would not be able to meet all their requests. The German council understood this and together we prioritized their requests and negotiated how we could meet which requests. Because both sides were willing to be flexible and to compromise, we created a compensation package that worked for our company and the German workers. Similar to the French Union, they wanted more pay and more time off, but they were willing to agree to work the number of hours that would allow us to provide these additional benefits.

The French and the German unions were both trying to do the best for their employees—that was their job. One came to the meeting with the intent of offering zero flexibility, zero compromise, and we all lost. The other was every bit as tough in their advocacy for their workers, but they were willing to employ flexibility to meet their workers' top priorities and negotiate on the lesser ones. Engaging in flexibility is a strength that requires the gathering of all available information, understanding the priorities of your company or those you represent and the realities of the situation, and then making the best decision for the company/people.

Being flexible doesn't mean that you must be flexible about everything. There will and should always be things you determine you cannot be flexible on. If you remember, in chapter 7, we decided not to move into Phase 4 of our last mile economic engine which was to expand globally. A big part of that decision was our unwillingness to be flexible with our value of the highest-quality service—we determined that we could not and would not adapt to providing good-enough service rather than great service to expand our business globally. We would arrive at that same juncture when we put our flexibility to the test with a new growth engine focused on fleet services for franchises.

Establishing Flexibility Parameters

Shortly after we launched last mile, we were approached by a few people who were in the leasing business of franchises, meaning they would contract with a franchisor like Taco Bell, Popeyes, or Jersey Mike's to provide fleet services to their franchisees (a franchisor owns and leases a licensed business model to a third party known as the franchisee). We were sold on the concept that we would sign with a franchisor that would enable us to contract fleets of 3,000–5,000 vehicles for their franchisees. We saw it as a promising new growth engine, and we hit the gas and took off. We hired three individuals who knew the franchise market well. One was a sales executive, another a sales manager, and the third was a bit of both sales and operations. We said to the new team and the company, "Okay, this is going to be different than what we've done before, but if we're flexible, we can really do this." We signed our first franchisor—let's call it ABC—and we were off and running.

The first ABC franchisee location called in for a cargo van. No problem, we told them, but because of the work they did, that $40,000 van they were looking to lease required an upfit of $10,000 to accommodate the materials they were transporting. We said, "That's okay, we're going to be flexible. Flexibility is one of the eight pillars of transformation after all—we got this."

The next ABC franchisee location called in for two vans, but they wanted slightly different vans than the first location's van. Flexibility is one of our values, "We got this," we reassured the client and ourselves. As challenges arose, our operations team would say, "Brendan, this is really hard," to which I would respond, "Great. It's really testing the boundaries of one of our five core values as a company: Flexibility. Remember, we want to provide great service, so let's think of innovative ways to deliver to small fleets."

As we progressed through this new growth engine, it was increasingly clear that the 3,000–5,000 vehicles we would be taking on through our contract with the franchisor would be broken up into a couple of unique vehicles spread out over more than two thousand franchise locations, and while the franchisee had to follow the vehicle branding requirements of the franchisor, they had some autonomy over what type, make, and adaptation their "fleet" would be composed of.

These individualized "fleets" of one or two vehicles were putting a strain on our service department who were equipped to service fleets of 500–15,000 of the same vehicle type, make, and model. As we continued to expand the franchise growth engine, our customer service people became overwhelmed by the number of requests for personalized service for their one or two vehicles. By the time we were six months in, our franchise clients were becoming the most difficult clients in the entire company to maintain.

That's when we first tapped the brakes and asked ourselves if we could really make this work. If, right now, we were challenged with only thirty locations and about one hundred vehicles, what would

happen when we had five hundred to one thousand of these locations with each of them calling in for personalized service for their two-vehicle fleets? As we continued to work at building our flexibility muscles, we also continued to listen and gather data. By months nine and ten, the data made it clear that we would never be able to provide that two-vehicle

customer in Billings, Montana, the same level of service as their local Enterprise, Budget, or Alamo could, because those companies were built to serve personal rental needs, which, in reality, was what each franchise location equated to.

That was when we really started to apply the brakes, and by the twelve-month mark, when we recognized that we were pushing the boundaries of one value, flexibility, at the expense of another value, service, we made the decision to put the car in park and move on from the franchise business.

When we communicated on our company-wide Zoom about our new economic engine business failure and exit from the franchise business, I thanked the team that had come in and helped us. I shared that we learned a lot of lessons. The most important ones being:

- We must remain flexible, but we must also establish clear parameters of our flexibility while continuing to provide high-quality service.
- We must honor all our values: one value cannot come at the expense of another—flexibility over service.
- It's okay to fail, and it's even better to talk about it.

The chat room on that company-wide Zoom lit up with references to *having the courage to fail and the faith to succeed*. What the franchise failure did successfully was confirm that, at Merchants, it's okay to try and fail. By sharing the failure, we also reinforced that when we fail, we won't hide from it; we'll talk about it and learn from it, together.

As a company transforms, they must be honest about what they are good at and what they are not good at, what fits their values and vision and what doesn't. When you identify what you are good at and it aligns with your values and vision, you must hit the gas pedal with both feet. When you identify what you're not good at, you must tap the brakes and take time to determine if you want to be good at it or if it's just not the right fit. When you assess if you have the capabilities to be good at it, you must ask, if, within the organization's people and culture, you have the right skills, the right attributes, and the right experience—and if you don't, can you upskill current new team members and/or hire new ones with what you need. If you decide it's simply not a good match, move on, but move on quickly and transparently.

At the time that we were attempting to build the franchise growth engine, we also saw the opportunity to venture into truck rental and decided to pursue that as well. Just as in the franchise segment, we would need to exercise flexibility if we were to be successful in the truck rental business—but this time, we were able to set the necessary flexibility parameters *and* be successful. Here's how it all played out.

We procured trucks—three different makes and models but every one of them white with zero upfitting and zero signage. We were not flexible on the color or any type of specialization. But our inflexibility on those things allowed us to be super flexible on rental terms. At the outset, we defined the flexibility of our parameters: rent any number of existing truck offerings as is for any number of months, anywhere in the country, and drive it anywhere you want to.

Those limited, but well-defined parameters were incredibly helpful to companies during the pandemic. During that time, we were approached by clients trying to navigate all the unknowns. When we were asked questions like, "I really want fifty new trucks on long-term leases, but I don't know how this COVID thing is going to turn out, so can I rent them for six months and then reassess?" we were able to respond with, "Absolutely! And if at the end of six months you want to extend your rental terms, we can do that or if you're ready to lease by then, we'll convert you to a long-term lease." We could not have had that level of flexibility with terms if we had chosen to also be flexible with colors, upfitting, and signage. And Merchants was the only player in the fleet industry offering that level of rental/lease options.

We were able to successfully build a small fleet growth engine in the truck rental business, because our parameters were that it had to be a homogenous vehicle. With a vehicle that wasn't flexible, we could provide flexible terms. In the franchise example, they wanted both a customized vehicle and flexible terms, and that's when we could no longer make it work. When they weren't in need of it, we couldn't easily offer it to a different customer who might be in construction, e-commerce, or higher ed, for example, like we could with the standardized ones.

We had seen opportunity in two markets, and we were flexible in both, but we could only maintain that level of flexibility *and* provide high-quality service in one of them.

While the franchise growth started, sputtered, and failed, our new last mile and truck rental growth engines that same year were wildly successful, and when team members talked to me about the experience that they learned the most from that year, it was the failure of the franchise business, because we had the opportunity to learn what we were *not* good at and what we were *incredibly* good at.

Transformational Flexibility

Transformational flexibility requires the willingness to see challenges as opportunities, the willingness to listen, the willingness to change, and the willingness to fail.

Let's break down each of these four components of transformational flexibility.

See Challenges as Opportunities

For leaders to see challenges as opportunities, they must consistently engage in a proactive and creative mindset. Here are some strategies to help you identify and leverage opportunities within challenges:

Stay in the Loop: Keep an eye on what's happening in your industry and what your customers are up to. Being aware of changes early on helps you get a head start in identifying potential challenges that could be leveraged as opportunities. Look both horizontally across your competitors and vertically throughout your supply chain. Keep a pulse and look for signals of change.

- *Think Growth:* See challenges as chances to make your business better. Instead of letting problems demotivate you and your team, flip them around and see them as opportunities to learn, get creative, and grow your business. When a challenging client is pushing you, view this as an opportunity to get better. When you are asked to perform a challenging task by a client, view this as an opportunity to grow your services. Whenever you hear your team say how "hard" or "impossible" something is, view that as something less likely to be done by your competitors which may just be a great growth opportunity for your company.

- *Dig into Your Data:* Be informed to understand what's working and what's not. Using data can help you spot trends, find areas for improvement, and reveal hidden opportunities within the challenges you face. Remember earlier when we were talking about leading indicators? Leading indicators are vitally important to seeing growth areas and opportunities. If you use your data well, you can weaponize it to be the point of the spear on many of your innovations.

- *Check Out the Competition:* See what other businesses are up to. If your competitors are facing challenges, that might be a chance for you to step in with a solution. It's a bit like finding a gap in the market. Remember when we talked about how Merchants competitors "hunkered down" during COVID, which meant there was a real opportunity to grab market share? This is an area that, quite simply, not enough companies put energy into or actively track. Keep in mind, with social media, podcasts, whitepapers, LinkedIn, and more, it is quite easy to see what your competitors are doing and who they are doing it with!

- *Get Creative:* Encourage your team to come up with new ideas. Brainstorming sessions, working together across different departments, and trying out new things can help you tackle challenges in an innovative way. Gamify your creativity, create a Shark Tank–like program in your company, keep conference rooms open with whiteboards, conduct meetings with the only agenda item being open discussion.

When we first began looking at truck rental as a new growth engine for Merchants, we needed to leverage our innovative culture to dig into our creativity and figure out all the *how will we* questions that began coming to the forefront.

"How will we store trucks currently not in service?" That question spurred a conversation about dealerships and automobile auction houses we could reach out to across the country—could we rent space from them? Which then spurred a conversation about what other services these potential storage providers might offer like maintenance and transportation services. It's energizing when your company's culture and people practice and promote a mindset of "We can do this, we just need to figure out how" and then explode into the collaborative energy of a brainstorming session. The truth is, today there isn't a service or product that can't be provided one way or the other. No matter what needs to be done, there is somebody who can do it. Don't believe me? Check out all the freelance sites like FIVER, Angi, Upwork, and more. If you need something done, someone will do it.

That's not to say it always should be done—remember, assessing gas or brake (and sometimes a full stop) is a continuous process. The next questions to be thought through included what our flexibility parameters were and if the solutions were repeatable (can its processes be replicated reliably to achieve consistent results) and scalable (can

the business handle the increase in growth without compromising efficiency or performance).

Now, let's step back into chapter 5 for a moment and review Pillar 3: People. Engaging in transformational flexibility requires the involvement of the right people with the right attributes—if you remember, high on that list was intellectual curiosity. The equation is simple: to see the opportunity in a challenge and how to successfully make that transition, you must be curious enough to wonder, "How can I/we make this happen?" If you don't have the right people with the right attributes—people with intellectual curiosity and the drive and ability to solve problems—challenges would simply remain challenges, and you'd never create enough accelerant to put the opportunity into motion.

Be Willing to Listen

As you lead your clients, team members, partners, third parties, and trusted stakeholders through a transition, you must be willing to listen to all of them. That doesn't mean you accommodate every request, but you must be willing to hear everyone's perspective, thoughts, and ideas. During a transformation, especially in the beginning stages, so much is in flux and often without a known solution. The best way to determine the winning solution often begins with listening. After all, your clients know what is and isn't working for them: your team members—if you've hired to your culture and skill and attribute needs—are equipped to find solutions; your vendors have experience, knowledge, and capabilities that can supplement your own; and your trusted stakeholders have a vested interest in your success. Listening, understanding, and acting upon the input gathered will strengthen the organization's ability to flex as needed.

While there are generalizations of how to actively listen, like focusing on what the person is saying without interrupting and showing that you're engaged through nods, eye contact, and verbal cues, I've broken down some best practices I've developed specific to each group.

- *Listening to Clients*
  - Clarify and Summarize: Repeat what you've heard to ensure you understand correctly. This not only confirms your understanding but also reassures the client that you value their input. And don't be surprised when after your end-of-meeting summary, your client decides to change some of their thoughts that they outlined minutes or hours earlier. Summarizing is a valuable tool that leads to better understanding. I encourage you to give it a try.

- Ask Open-Ended Questions: Encourage clients to share more by asking open-ended questions. This helps you uncover their needs, preferences, and concerns in greater detail.
- Empathy: Put yourself in your client's shoes to understand their perspective and emotions. Demonstrating empathy builds trust and rapport.
- Feedback Mechanisms: Establish clear channels for feedback. Regularly seek opinions on your products or services to ensure you stay aligned with client expectations. At Merchants, we do this in a big way with our Client Summits that I shared with you in chapter 4 under Pillar 2: Culture (see how closely all the pillars are connected!).

- *Listening to Team Members*

  - Open-Door Policy: Create an environment where team members feel comfortable sharing their thoughts and concerns. An open-door policy encourages open communication.
  - Regular Check-Ins: Schedule regular one-on-one meetings to discuss both work-related matters and personal development. This builds a deeper understanding of each team member. At Merchants, we augmented our "one-on-one check-ins" with regular employee huddles and our annual leadership and employee summits.
  - Active Participation: Actively participate in team meetings. Show that you value and consider the input of each team member. Remember we began with Transformational Leadership as the first pillar? Well, without our

leaders committed to actively participating and listening in team meetings, the innovation necessary to fuel our economic engines would have stalled early on.

▫ Recognition: Acknowledge and appreciate team members' contributions in big and small ways. Feeling heard and recognized boosts morale.

- *Listening to Partners and Vendors*

    ▫ Regular Communication: Maintain open lines of communication with your vendors. Regular updates and check-ins foster a cooperative relationship and can head off problems before they arise. Partners and vendors also have relationships across your industry and provide you signals of what others are doing in your market.

    ▫ Long-Term Vision: Discuss long-term goals and visions with your vendors. This is one of my personal favorites. Instead of telling our vendors what they need to do for us or assuming we know all that they can do, I invited them to Merchants and began the conversation with, "If you want to grow your business with Merchants, tell us about all of your capabilities." This discourse lays the foundation for a collaborative partnership: a partnership that will be flexible with you as you grow.

    ▫ Clear Expectations: Clearly communicate your expectations and ask for theirs. Understanding each other's needs helps prevent misunderstandings.

    ▫ Feedback Loops: Encourage vendors to provide feedback on your collaboration. This two-way communication can lead to improvements in your partnership.

- *Listening to Trusted Stakeholders*
    - Stakeholder Surveys: Conduct regular surveys to gather feedback from stakeholders. This data-driven approach provides insights into their perspectives. At Merchants, we had a multi-prong approach. Three key areas included: (1) we conducted banker meetings with our bank group and had them complete surveys, (2) we created a small group of clients that provided deeper input with us on a semi-annual basis, and (3) we invited third parties to our board meetings to provide feedback on our strategy, brand, and leadership. There are so many ways to accomplish this, but it all starts with the willingness to listen.
    - Transparency: Be transparent about your business decisions and their impact. This fosters trust and shows stakeholders that their input is valued.
    - Advisory Groups: Establish advisory groups with key stakeholders. Their collective insights can guide decision-making processes.

Be Willing to Change

An organization's willingness to change sets the foundation for its flexibility. Trust me, your industry, client needs, and competitors are changing, so if you are just standing still, you're not simply maintaining the status quo; you're moving backward. To transform, a company must cultivate a culture that embraces change and is flexible enough to adjust quickly to those changes.

When an organization demonstrates its willingness to change by embracing and empowering:

- An attitude and mindset of being open to potential shifts in strategies, processes, or structures.
- A proactive approach to recognizing external factors that may impact the business and a readiness to respond appropriately.
- A culture that embraces new ideas and technologies to foster innovation, values learning, welcomes feedback, and sees change as an opportunity for growth.
- Opportunities to acknowledge and take calculated risks to explore new possibilities or address challenges.
- A commitment to meeting client needs and expectations, even if it requires adapting business practices or offerings.
- The ability to remain humble and admit when you are going about something in a wrong way or manner—it's amazing how far humility goes when pushing for change.

It lays the foundation for the level of flexibility that will enable the organization to:

- Implement innovative solutions and continuously improve its processes, products, or services based on feedback and changing market dynamics.
- Navigate unforeseen challenges by adjusting strategies and operations swiftly, minimizing the impact of risks.
- Respond to changing customer preferences and market demands, ensuring that products or services remain relevant.
- Ensure that strategic plans are adaptable, allowing the organization to pivot when necessary, without compromising its overall objectives.
- Capitalize on emerging trends, outmaneuver competitors, and stay ahead in a rapidly changing market.

Be Willing to Fail

Now, we arrive at the final piece of the transformational flexibility puzzle: the willingness to fail. I want to stress again that flexibility is not about saying yes to every opportunity or every request. Flexibility is about the willingness to see challenges as opportunities, to listen, and to change and then assess what opportunities and changes are in the organization's best interests and establish the flexibility parameters required for their success. As an example, let's expand on the truck rental growth engine I discussed earlier in the chapter.

Year 1 of our truck rental venture, we went to market with three brands of white, quarter-ton pickup trucks. In Year 2, we expanded our go-to-market offerings by adding a half-ton and three-quarter-ton pickup truck, and in Year 3, our go-to-market offerings included flatbed trucks, step vans, and tractor trailers. Each new go-to-market

offering aligned with our flexibility parameters of white, no uplift, and no signage trucks.

Now, if someone had asked us for a three-quarter-ton or flatbed truck the first year we rolled out truck rental, we would have had to say no, because to offer these trucks nationally, we needed to have 1,500 of each type of truck (quarter-ton, half-ton, three-quarter-ton, and flatbed) across the country, and we were not positioned to do that in Year 1.

If, at the starting gate of our truck rental business, we had hit the gas on all these truck offerings, we would have failed. We needed to be able to amass and assess in phases. By the end of Year 3, we discovered that there just wasn't the market for flatbeds that we thought there was, and we pulled out of that segment.

While our quarter-ton, half-ton, and three-quarter-ton truck rental business continues to be highly successful, our flatbed rental was a bust. But that's okay because we went into all of it with a willingness to fail. You see, an individual, team, or company can be willing to see challenges as opportunities to listen, and to change, but none of those will matter if they aren't also willing to fail, because nothing is a sure bet. To try anything new like reading, riding a bike, driving a car, or creating a new economic engine, one must be willing to fail in the course of their learning and trying.

When you're tapping the brakes to assess how well your strategy, growth engine, system, initiative, etc. is working and the data indicates it won't be successful, work quickly to determine whether adjustments can be made to ensure success or if you need to hit the brakes, full stop, and shut it down, because if you're going to fail, the best thing you can do is fail as fast as possible, learn from it, and move on. I realize this is not always easy to do. Depending on how personally invested you are in something's success, it can be super challenging to let it go—even when you know that's what needs to be done.

Here's what I've found to be the key: don't let the "thing" (last mile, truck rental, franchises, fill in the blank) become your identity. Instead, let your identity be that of innovative thinker, transformer, and disruptive creator, because that person manages their EQ and IQ to make the tough decisions with intelligence and care and recognizes that what they are creating, disrupting, and transforming is bigger than themselves and not limited to one singular success or failure.

Let me ask you, when was the last time you successfully failed?

The willingness to fail and fail fast is a great segue to our final chapter, Pillar 8: Fearlessness. Leading fearlessly is not charging over a cliff; leading fearlessly is about laying the groundwork so that you, your team, and your company are equipped to navigate the challenges and seize the opportunities that come your way.

The groundwork for fearless, transformational leadership? You guessed it—everything we've just covered:

- Pillar 1: Leadership
- Pillar 2: Culture
- Pillar 3: People
- Pillar 4: Systems
- Pillar 5: IQ
- Pillar 6: EQ
- Pillar 7: Flexibility

Without the right leadership, you can't cultivate the right culture; without the right culture, you can't recruit, train, and retain the right people; without the right people, you can't build the right systems; and when those things don't happen, all the IQ, EQ, and flexibility a leader can muster isn't going to lead to a successful transformation. Why? Because the IQ, EQ, and flexibility required for transformation must be fundamentally woven into the leadership, culture, people, and systems.

They are all interconnected and critical to the process. But they alone are not enough for a company to transform.

But what does make a good transformation GREAT or a disruptive idea SPECIAL? A healthy dose of fearlessness. So, what do you say? Let's jump into fearlessness together.

CHAPTER 10

PILLAR 8: FEARLESSNESS

By now, you've figured out I am a huge sports fan. Among my favorite sports to follow is Formula 1 racing. What really drew me in as a superfan was what Zak Brown's fearless leadership has done for the McLaren team. When Brown came on board in 2016, it was on the heels of McLaren's worst year in the organization's history. Once the second most successful team in the history of the sport, McLaren finished ninth out of ten in the 2015 constructor standings—their worst ranking since 1983.

Right out of the gate, Brown began building McLaren's new leadership team which would serve as the foundation on which he would return McLaren to the top of the leaderboard.

It's been thrilling to watch Zak transform the leadership, culture, people, and systems at McLaren to make it all come together. But it is Zak's fearlessness that has inspired me the most.

From making what he said was one of his toughest decisions, breaking away from McLaren's veteran driver, Daniel Ricciardo, in the middle of 2022 and betting on a rookie, Oscar Piastri, who had never raced in F1, to building McLaren's very own state-of-the-art wind tunnel in response to the industry's new salary cap, Brown continues to lead his team fearlessly forward. That fearlessness has put McLaren back near the top of the leaderboard—finishing fourth in the 2023 constructors' standings and, as of the writing of this book, looking up to P3 for 2024.

The first thing I needed to do was transform my leadership team into one filled with excellent, transparent communicators, so we could begin to rebuild that trust.

—Zak Brown[19]

Formula 1 racing is a very public industry, and as such, Zak has faced tremendous judgment and pushback from his detractors. In fact, the 2023 season got off to a very slow start and as documented in the Netflix series *Drive to Survive*, Zak's job was on the line. But as a true fearless leader, he held to the pillars of disruptive transformation and his contagious leadership style to turn the team around by mid-season and close strong. Through it all, he has remained steadfast in his vision for McLaren and continues to lead fearlessly every step of the way.

When you're the leader, when you're called upon for that transformation, you must take in all the data analytics, regression models, scenario planning, and expert advice, but you must also accept their limitations. There is no analytical model or industry expert who can guarantee which direction you should head in. To disrupt and

---

19   Brendan P. Keegan, *The FUD Factor* (Forbes Books), https://books.forbes.com/ books/the-fud-factor/.

transform, it is incumbent on the leader to activate their fearlessness to forge the right path forward. Your fearlessness as a leader will empower others to activate their own fearlessness and begin forging the path alongside you.

So often, taking that first leap is the hardest; we're uncertain of the results and we begin to doubt our own abilities and judgment.

I think most of us can relate to the kid who walks to the end of the diving board and stands there battling their fear, trying to muster the courage to take the plunge. But once the splash landing is made, and they've popped back up for air, the kid is pumped because not only did they find the courage to push past their fear and survive the jump, but they also realize that it was so much less scary and difficult than they imagined it would be. Now, they're scrambling out of the pool and scurrying up the ladder so they can do it again and again and again. And with each new level of confidence, they're trying new dives or maybe a higher board, pushing the boundaries of their fearlessness.

Facing your fears at the end of the diving board works the same way when you're standing on the precipice of transforming a business, starting a new division, or changing your product; until you start doing it, you're always going to be at the end of that diving board. Sometimes, we can activate our own fearlessness and jump off, other times we need one or two or ten people cheering us on the sideline before we muster the courage to take the plunge, and then, there are times when we simply need a good friend (or enemy) to just push us off the edge.

How long have you been standing at the end of the diving board?

The FUD Factor

What is FUD? It's the fear, uncertainty, and doubt that we must all overcome to achieve what seems impossible, whether that's jumping off the diving board, accepting a new job, seeing our child off on their very first day of school, or transforming a business. We all experience fear, uncertainty, and doubt as we go about our days and our lives— that's normal and a good thing, because fearlessness is not about being reckless (we'll say more on that later). But to live our lives fully, to achieve all that we can achieve, we must push ourselves beyond our fear, uncertainty, and doubt, and as a fearless leader, we must help those we are leading do the same.

Throughout Merchants' transformation, I have had the privilege of witnessing so many of our team members overcome their FUD and go on to achieve more than they ever imagined they could. Let me share a couple of stories.

One of Merchants' leaders, who had been with the company many years, was incredibly capable but also highly resistant to change. Before I came on board, the culture had been one of maintaining the status quo, of not deviating from a successful status quo strategy. Trying something new and failing was not an option. I understood this leader's FUD around stepping outside of the box that he had been put in. He didn't know me. He had no idea if I even knew what I was talking about when I pushed for our new last mile and truck rental growth engines. He also didn't know that just because I said he wouldn't be fired if he tried something new and it failed that I would be true to my word if that failure came to fruition. He was standing at the end of the proverbial diving board, and it took time to build the trust that would eventually empower him to jump off.

While he never said no to doing what I asked, he would be slow to take each step, because he would want to gather enough data that would confirm it was the right step to take. What should have taken a week, took a month, and what should have taken a month, took four months. When you're trying to transform, the inability to make decisions and move quickly is the kiss of death, because disruptive transformations are about accelerating faster and being more disruptive than your competitors. About six months into the transformation, I remember having a conversation with him where I said, "You are person A," and I drew A on the whiteboard. "And you like to grow 5 percent a year," and I wrote 5 percent next to A. "I'm looking for person B," and I wrote B on the whiteboard. "They grow between 50–100 percent a year," and I wrote 50–100 percent next to B. "And now let me introduce you to person C." I wrote C on the whiteboard. "Do you know who person C is?"

"Is that my new boss?" he asked.

"Well, it is if they decide to keep you," I replied. "I need you to become person B. You have all the attributes and abilities, but there's one thing holding you back: fear. You're deathly afraid of making a decision you haven't made before, because you rely so much on your past experiences and 'definitive' data that just doesn't exist. And now, I'm asking you to make decisions on truck rental and last mile—things you haven't done before—which clearly makes you uncomfortable, and that discomfort makes you hesitate. There's no room for hesitation in a transformation. Transformation requires decisiveness. I need you to be decisive, and that will require you to overcome your personal fears."

That conversation was a turning point, and once he channeled his strengths to overcome his fears, he leapt off the diving board and never looked back. In four years, he went from leading the generation of two million in revenue to over one hundred million in revenue, and more importantly, he became Merchants' number one fearless leader coach, empowering everyone he leads to move fearlessly forward. This leader had completely transformed personally which in turn led to the transformation of his business. He was truly amazing to watch.

Now, let me tell you about another special person who required a bit of time and coaxing to adjust to this overcoming FUD thing. Remember the chairman I talked about at the very beginning of the book and my breakfast in the diner? Well, he was 100 percent on board the transformation race car, but there were times we needed to bring the company in for a pitstop and patiently walk through why we were doing what we were doing. The chairman's perspective was less about fear and more about uncertainty. We were doing things that he had never seen before, and it was more a question of not understanding the how and why of what we were doing than it was a fear of what we were doing. One of my favorite moments of nearly every meeting with the chairman was this: "Hey Brendan what are the odds of this being successful? 50–50?" The surest way to discuss uncertainty with the chairman was to set the conversation up as a "bet." To help him embrace change, we needed to speak his language—we needed to provide solid and clear communication if he wanted to join us on the journey.

Being a fearless leader is making calculated decisions without the guarantee of success—like placing a bet. Fearlessness is all about taking a risk that may fail but notice that the risk is based on *calculated* decisions, because what fearlessness is not is reckless. Merchants' fearless leaps into new markets, new asset classes, and new EVs are great examples.

Fearlessness Is Not Recklessness

As I shared in chapter 7, in 2021, because we saw EVs as a key cog in the future of fleets, we made a commitment to reserve forty thousand EVs (a $2 billion commitment) so that by 2025, 50 percent of our mobility fleet would be EVs, and by 2030, 50 percent of our entire fleet would be EVs. Some people questioned if we were blurring the lines between being fearless and being reckless. While it certainly required fearlessness to distinguish Merchants as the most disruptive company in our industry and the leader in fleet EVs, I would argue that it was not reckless. Here's why.

Our agreements were to reserve, not buy, forty thousand EVs. That meant we had first right of refusal on these vehicles when they became available without a hard commitment to buy. This was possible because the EV builders were also being fearless without being reckless. If they required a commitment to buy, they would be committed to a delivery schedule without room to adjust to market and policy changes that could significantly impact the EV industry. They would also be committed to specifications of vehicles that had not been built yet and locked into prices that were still unknown.

Fast-forward three years, and in 2024, in North America, the launch of EVs has slowed down due to a variety of factors. First, the post-COVID impact on auto manufacturing's supply chain, followed by two years of historic inflation and the slow progress on the U.S. EV infrastructure network. Merchants and the EV OEMs never backed off from our fearlessness to move into the EV market, but our fearlessness had to adjust to the American consumers and commercial entities' fluctuating commitment to EVs. This has translated into downshifting our EV engines and slowing the influx of vehicles, but not abandoning the strategy. Merchants, the EV manufacturers, and the EV infrastructure players have all worked together to slow our roll into electrification.

This eighth pillar, Fearlessness, requires continuous testing against each of the seven pillars before it. As we moved forward on our EV commitment, we had to assess against each pillar in the following ways.

- Pillar 1: Leadership: We needed to expand our leadership team and bring in external leaders who understood the engineering side of EVs. And our existing leaders needed to "go back to school" and learn a new EV playbook that our new leaders created.

- Pillar 2: Culture: Our culture embraced the EV gamble with passion, but we also needed to ensure our culture didn't get out in front of the strategic decision and begin to move recklessly. One of the upsides of creating a great innovative culture is that it innovates. We needed to keep the reins on the innovative aspect of our culture and move at the pace of the American fleet buyer.

- Pillar 3: People: As we expanded our leadership team and our strategic thinking, we needed our people to think in new ways and we also needed to add to the rank and file. The good news was that we had people excited to embrace the new vehicle technology.

- Pillar 4: Systems: As a technology-based company, our systems needed to adjust and take into account a new type of vehicle. One with different properties and supply chains. Our systems needed to change and be flexible.

- Pillar 5: IQ: With each decision time requiring a yes or no to the next batch of reserved EVs, we tapped into our IQ to assess the market signals that would enable us to make a calculated decision. Did the last grouping of EVs lease successfully or were they still sitting on our lot? If we hadn't been able to move them, why? Consumer sentiment has changed due to lack of an effective EV infrastructure—what would that mean for Merchants?

- Pillar 6: EQ: Our emotional intelligence was challenged—there was a part of us as leaders that wondered, "Are we out in front too much?" and "Are we predicting the future correctly?" We needed to be incredibly self-aware. Whenever you challenge your own self-awareness, there are some uncomfortable moments, and we were not immune.

- Pillar 7: Flexibility: Perhaps one of the most critical pillars was being flexible, and our flexibility was tested in ways we never expected. There were times our collective IQ gave the green light to be super flexible in unique ways. Other times, it told us there was zero room for flexibility. That roller coaster of a disparate flexibility range tested us frequently.

Fearlessness Is the Willingness to Fail and Fail Fast

I've talked about the need for decisiveness when acting fearlessly—the longer you stand at the edge of the diving board trying to convince yourself to take the leap, the less likely you are to leap. Once you've decided to climb the ladder and walk to the edge, you must be willing to jump, or if you assess the risk is too great, abort immediately. That fearless decisiveness is just as critical when it's time to pull the plug as it is when it's all systems go. If when you get to the edge of the board, you realize the water is too low for you to jump safely, your decision to abort the jump must be immediate. The same is true in business; when it's clear that failure is imminent, you must fail as fast as possible.

"Failing fast" in business refers to the practice of quickly identifying and acknowledging when a particular approach, strategy, or product isn't working as expected and then pivoting or abandoning it in favor of trying something else. The idea is to fail quickly, learn from the experience, and iterate rapidly to find the most effective solution or path forward.

For a company to do this successfully, they must cultivate a culture in which failing is not only okay but encouraged. Here are four key strategies to assure your team members that failure is okay and in fact essential to your success.

1. *Build Trust:* Employees must feel empowered to take risks and try new things without fear of negative consequences or punishment if they don't succeed.

2. *Communicate Openly:* Communication must be open and transparent at all levels of the organization, creating an environment where people feel comfortable sharing their ideas, opinions, and failures without judgment.

3. *Emphasize Learning:* Failure must be seen as an opportunity for growth and learning rather than something to be avoided at all costs. Employees must be encouraged to reflect on their failures, extract valuable lessons, and apply them to future endeavors.

4. *Value Innovation:* The organization must demonstrate that it values experimentation and innovation by investing time and resources into trying new approaches, even if they carry a risk of failure.

Cultivating a culture of innovation and the willingness to fail doesn't end there. You must not only role model the process for working through failure, but you must involve the appropriate team members in the process. Here are some tips on how to successfully commit to failing.

1. *Openly Acknowledge the Failure:* Accept that the failure has occurred and take responsibility for it. Avoid making excuses or blaming others.

2. *Adapt and Act:* Use the insights gained from the failure to identify adjustments to your approach or strategy and take action.

3. *Learn from the Experience:* Reflect on what went wrong and why. Identify the factors that contributed to the failure and the lessons that can be learned from it.

4. *Remain Resilient:* Failure is a natural part of the learning process, and it's important to remain resilient in the face of setbacks. Stay focused on your goals and continue moving forward, even in the face of adversity.

Trust me when I tell you, successfully failing fast will benefit you and your company tremendously. Here are just a few of those benefits.

1. *Efficient Resource Allocation:* By quickly identifying and abandoning unsuccessful approaches, you can avoid wasting time and resources on endeavors that are unlikely to succeed.

2. *Faster Innovation:* Failing fast allows you to iterate rapidly and experiment with new ideas, leading to faster innovation and adaptation to changing market conditions.

3. *Improved Decision-Making:* Embracing failure as a learning opportunity encourages employees to take calculated risks and make decisions more confidently.

4. *Competitive Advantage:* Embracing a culture of failing fast enables agility and adaptability, giving you a competitive edge in rapidly evolving industries.

Netflix is an industry giant that has reaped the benefits of successfully failing fast time and time again. In chapter 1, I compared the success of Netflix against Blockbuster's failure. Netflix was able to transform and disrupt the industry while Blockbuster went bust. Blockbuster played it safe with what they knew, while Netflix continually experimented with new ways for its customers to watch movies: they were willing to try and fail. Today, Netflix is well known for its fail fast philosophy. As a streaming service, they have fully embraced the opportunity to constantly measure what their viewers are watching and how they are watching it in real time. If a show fails to pull in the views or hit their goals, they'll drop it and reallocate resources to other projects.

This ability to fail fast and pivot has allowed Netflix to stay relevant in the constantly changing entertainment landscape and maintain its position as a leader in the streaming industry. So invested in failing as an integral part of success, CEO Reed Hastings once warned that Netflix's "hit ratio was too high," and that they had to "take more risk" and "try more crazy things because we should have a higher cancel rate overall."[20]

Google is another industry giant who attributes success to a willingness to fail. Because it is embedded in everything they do, Google is known not just for its products and services, but for its famously cool, risk-taking, and innovative culture. Google has nine Principles of Innovation, two of which speak directly to the importance of trying and failing.

- *Launch and Iterate:* Ship your products out to market early and often rather than waiting until they are absolutely perfect to take them to market. The most important button on any product is the feedback button.

---

20   Nathan McAlone, "Netflix CEO Reed Hastings wants to start canceling more shows – here's why," June 3, 2017, https://www.businessinsider.com/netflix-wants-to-start-canceling-a-lot-more-shows-2017-6.

- *Fail Well:* If you don't fail often, you're not pushing the boundaries of innovation. Failure is a badge of honor. Be honest about it and fail with pride.[21]
- *To put it simply:* without risk and failure, there is no learning, and without learning, there is nothing new to lead. To truly lead fearlessly, you must be willing to try and fail often. You must be willing to face your FUD in everything you do.

Be Fearless in Everything

At Merchants, we intentionally chose to bet on our young leaders. As we discovered in chapter 3, experience and skills alone do not make the leader. I would argue that attributes carry the biggest weight in determining someone's leadership abilities. Experience and skills can be taught. Attributes cannot so much be taught but cultivated in the person who is naturally inclined toward those attributes. Regardless of our age and experience, we all have attributes that impact how we move in the world. These are the four attributes that I previously shared, which I believe are critical for a fearless leader:

- Intellectual curiosity
- Open-mindedness
- Collaboration
- Trust

When we began to look at our young potential leaders, we looked beyond skills and experience and delved into their attributes: Do they ask why? Are they flexible and collaborative? Do others seek them out?

---

21 Dan Croitor, "Google's 9 principles of innovation via Kamal Haasan, Larry page, Shannon Deegan & Sundar Pichai," https://www.youtube.com/watch?v=Q7bl3oc17UM.

Do they listen openly to the perspective of others? Are they decisive? Are they willing to take calculated risks? As we began to look at our younger team members in new ways, there were several who clearly had what it took to be a fearless leader and needed the opportunity to develop their skills and expand their experience.

One of those young leaders had started with the company in college. Within two years of our transformation, when he was in his late twenties, he accepted a VP role in the company even though he didn't have the breadth of experience his VP colleagues did nor the full technical expertise the role required. What he had in spades was the natural and acquired leadership attributes, and we knew, with the company's support, he would develop the experience and skills over time.

Two years into serving successfully in his VP role overseeing a division of one hundred team members, we pulled him out and asked him to start up a new division in which, at least initially, he would not supervise anyone. Now, many people would have at the very least hesitated at giving up a role in charge of one hundred people to start a new division of one. Some would have said, "Brendan, thank you for the offer to do this new job, but I just don't think it's, for me, and I'm going to stay where I'm at." And that would've been perfectly acceptable, but this young man proved to be as fearless as we thought he would be.

"If that's what the company needs me to do, I'll absolutely do it" was his unflinching response.

Now, we assured him that in taking this leap, we would be there to provide support and resources, and that if things didn't go well, we would also have his back and find another role in the company for him. He didn't need our help to be fearless in his willingness to take on a new opportunity—that was natural for him, but demonstrating we trusted in his abilities and that we were there to support him every step of the way vanquished any doubts or uncertainties about his lack of experience and skills.

He excelled in his new role, and by the second year of starting the new division, he had a seat on the senior leadership team alongside peers who were twenty and thirty years older. The company bet on his talent, but most importantly, he bet on his own fearlessness.

It is a leader's responsibility to identify people who are demonstrating the motivation and willingness to lead and provide them with the opportunity to excel, to be fearless, and to lead. When you choose to mentor and pass on your fearlessness, the ripple effect is immeasurable. Once someone demonstrates fearlessness—once they leap off that diving board and emerge energized—it spreads like wildfire, and the desire to overcome fears is ignited in those around us. Before you know it, you've inspired ten people to jump off that diving board, and each of those ten people inspire ten more people, and on and on and on. And that's just the beginning.

What I'm about to say now is as important as anything else I've shared in this book. *Once you fearlessly take that leap off the diving board, your transformational leadership journey doesn't end.* In fact, that first leap is just the beginning. Transformational leadership requires continual attention to and effort in every one of the eight pillars I have laid out for you. The moment you stop, you fall behind, and one day you'll hear a team member say, "Remember when we transformed, remember when we fearlessly conquered last mile, remember when …" rather than, "Let's do (fill in the blank)!"

Transforming, disrupting, and leading fearlessly is an evolving process that you must continually breathe life into. Remember in chapter 3, when I talked about bringing in three leaders from outside the industry and three leaders from our competitors to complement the knowledge and skills of Merchants' existing leaders? Well, guess what? Six years later, we had to do it all over again. This time, bringing in two new leaders from outside the industry and two new leaders from our competitors. We took this step because it's critical that new ideas and ways of thinking are continuously funneled into the company. It is natural over time, for everyone to meld into the "company's" way of thinking, and when that happens, stagnation is close behind.

Transformational leadership is not linear; it is a continuous cycle of improving and connecting each of the eight pillars to successfully achieve the impossible.

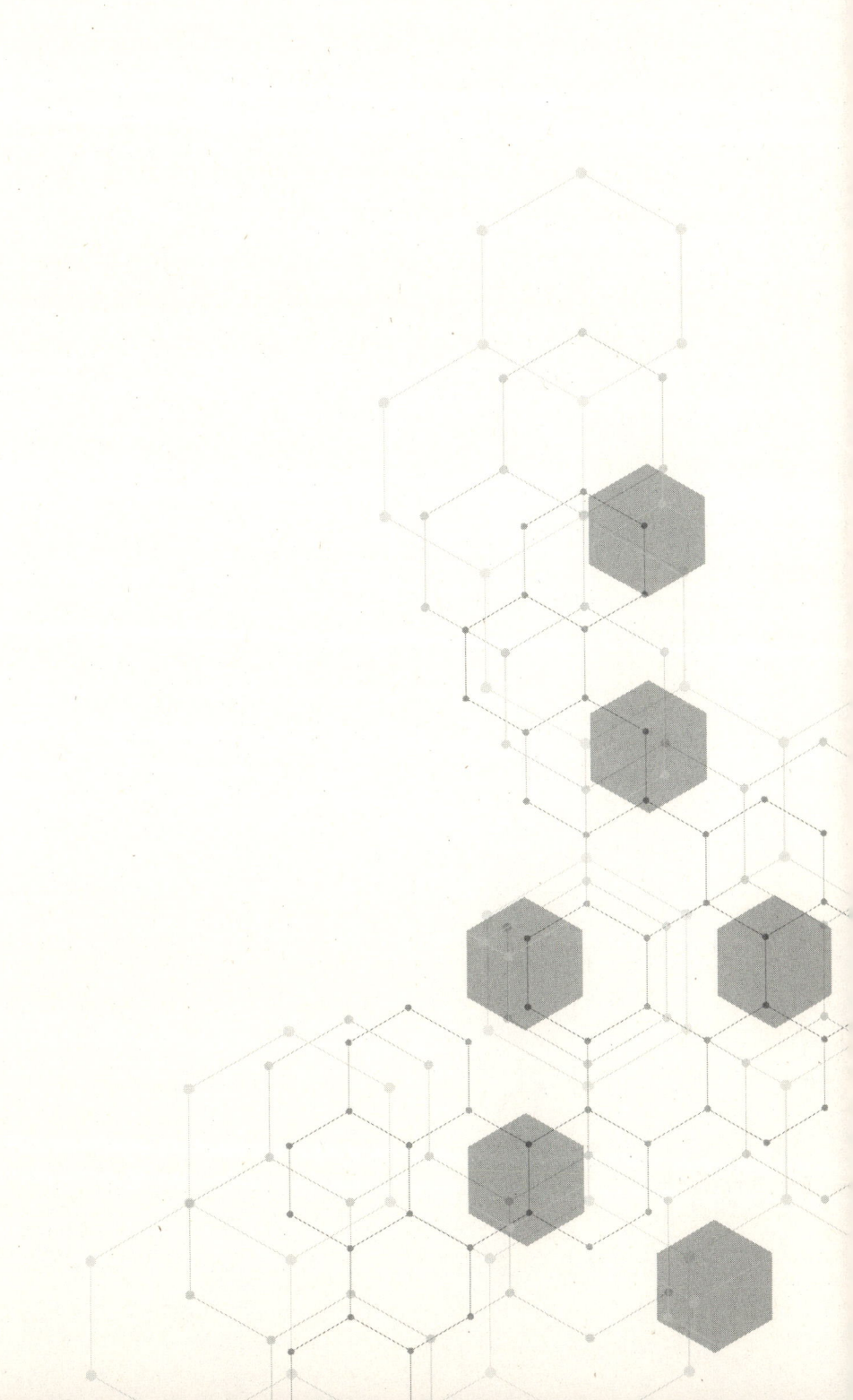

WE WERE TOLD IT COULDN'T BE DONE. WE DID IT ANYWAY!

It was set to be a normal Friday 8:00 a.m. call with our lead financial partner. We were thirty days into COVID, 90 percent of our employees were all safely working from home, we were keeping our clients' fleets on the road, and our mantra was *Keep America Moving*.

One hundred and twenty seconds into the call, our financial partner's message was clear and to the point. "There is no money in the market for you, your clients, or your growth. Stay liquid and stop your funding. We are pens down—there is nothing we can do for you."

My team hung up their phones from different locations, and I sent out a Zoom video-conference invite for an internal meeting at 8:05 a.m. During those few minutes, my mind raced. I thought through our options and quickly realized we only had one.

231

As the video feeds came online and the stunned looks on my team members' faces popped into view, I informed them that we would stay the course, continue funding, and launch a campaign that we were open for business. There was money in the market—we would just need to work twice as hard to find it. We would not be following our lead financial partner's advice. They were focused on all their clients who were struggling due to the pandemic. At Merchants, we would focus on our opportunities—we would Dare to DISRUPT!

Now, before I walk you through how we succeeded, I want to provide you with a bit of context. The pandemic was first and foremost on everyone's mind, and in reaction to this unknown, companies in most industries, as well as investors, were holding on tight to whatever cash was on hand. From the bank's point of view, it was the epitome of a non-spending market. This was true in our sector, too. The fleet industry overall saw a dip in revenue of close to 40 percent, and many of our competitors had stopped funding.

At the time, not everyone understood that our company was on the precipice of a tremendous growth opportunity. Growth, like team momentum in sports, is the culmination of many factors, some of which are out of everyone's direct control. Growth isn't just about having a good product or service. It's also about the market, the competition, the company culture, and the people around you.

If we followed the advice we were given and hit the "off" switch in terms of funding existing clients and acquiring new ones, it's entirely possible that we wouldn't be able to turn it back on. I wasn't willing to take that chance. The bottom line was that we saw the opportunity for growth, we knew we needed funding to support the growth, and our bank wasn't willing to support us. Boy, did they make the wrong decision.

Over the next twelve months, we raised a total of $370 million from other banks and investment firms that believed in our disruption story. They fed off our daring nature, and it became contagious. In fact, we grew the company $378 million that year, took great care of our clients, and secured some new ones in the process. So, you might be doing the math right now, we grew more than we raised capital—this is true. The market bought into our innovation, our culture, our transformation, and when you get people and institutions to buy in, good things follow, and so the money and capital flowed in from all corners of the world—Asia, Europe, and North America.

None of that would have been possible if we hadn't already established our Leadership foundation upon which we were able to build our Culture, People, Systems, IQ, EQ, and Flexibility, all of which ultimately fueled our Fearlessness to take that incredible leap off the proverbial diving board that day.

So, what lessons can I share with you about leading a transformation during the craziest of times when nothing was certain?

Lesson 1: Run the Playbook

Hopefully *Dare to Disrupt* has given you a framework for leading a transformation through the eight pillars. No matter how challenging, or what changes, or what's going on in the world, run the playbook—it works.

Lesson 2: Value Your Employees with Education and Transparency

Your team members can take your company to heights you never even imagined. The key is to speak, act, and think with transparency and constantly work to educate your employees on why you are doing what you are doing.

Lesson 3: Short-Term Pain for Long-Term Gain

You will take lots of hits, bumps, and bruises as you transform. That's okay. It's part of the process. In fact, to truly transform in the long term, you must try lots of new things with hits and misses, ups and downs, wild successes, and total failures. But don't let the short-term pain ever get you down.

Lesson 4: Be Daring

Believe in yourself. Believe in your teammates. Believe in your clients. And be daring and bold in your approach.

FEARLESS DISRUPTION

Disruption is a team sport, which is why the journey and our relationship don't stop when you put this book down. I invite you to continue the conversation with me on the below channels where you can find free content, including tips, programs, podcasts, articles, and information on how we can stay connected, share thoughts, and learn while continuing our relationship.

Let's stay connected:

Website	brendanpkeegan.com
Email	b@brendanpkeegan.com
LinkedIn	https://www.linkedin.com/in/brendanpkeegan/
Instagram	@bpkFEARLESS
Facebook	@bpkFEARLESS
Twitter	@bpkFEARLESS
Podcast	forbesbooksaudio.com/shows/fearless-leadership/